Praise for This Book

"A how-to classic."
—*The Washington Post*

"An invaluable tool, infinitely wise and very practical.
No businessperson should be without this handy guide."
—Kenneth S. Olshan,
chairman of the board and CEO,
Wells Rich Greene BDDP, Inc.

"The basis of all motivation is communication. To be a successful
communicator requires discipline, understanding, and verve.
Joan Detz understands this and provides a firm foundation
from which to launch influential communications."
—James S. Todd, M.D.,
executive vice president,
the American Medical Association

"This book is a practical text for helping anyone develop the
ability to speak and to become more effective."
—Terrence J. McCann,
executive director,
Toastmasters International

"In international business, knowing how to speak efficiently and
effectively is the key to success. This handy book will help busy
executives master this important skill."
—Dr. Mitsuru Misawa, president,
Industrial Bank of Japan Leasing (USA) Inc., and
director, IBJ Leasing (Tokyo)

How to Write &
Give a Speech

Other Books by Joan Detz

You Mean I Have to Stand Up & Say Something?
Can You Say a Few Words?
It's Not What You Say, It's How You Say It

How to Write & Give a Speech

Second Revised Edition

A Practical Guide for Executives, PR People, the Military, Fund-raisers, Politicians, Educators, and Anyone Who Has to Make Every Word Count

Joan Detz

St. Martin's Griffin New York

www.stmartins.com

Design by Tanya M. Pérez

ISBN 0-312-30273-8

10   9   8   7   6   5   4

This book is dedicated to the people
who have attended my speechwriting seminars over the years.
They come from diverse work backgrounds—
from corporations and universities,
to the U.S. Congress and our nation's armed forces.
But they leave with one important thing in common—a
respect for the value, and the power, of the spoken word.
They write speeches that make a difference.
I applaud them.

Contents

Acknowledgments

This is the second revised edition of *How to Write & Give a Speech*—and I owe gratitude to many people.

Certainly, I want to start by thanking my editor, Marian Lizzi. Marian knows what's important in a book—and she works to make it happen. I value her editorial direction and her integrity.

In a larger sense, I want to thank my publisher. The truth is, St. Martin's Press believed in the value of this book long before anyone else did. They bought it back in 1983 on the basis of a three-page proposal—and nothing gives me more pleasure than seeing my publisher get a well-deserved return on their investment! In an era marked by shifting business loyalties, St. Martin's Press has consistently treated me well—and I am proud to have them publish my books.

I also want to thank my literary agent, Peter Miller. Two decades ago he read my proposal, took me to lunch, and said the most wonderful words any author could hear: "I want to sell this book for you." Peter, you did it, and I remember.

It was Dominic Chianese (a.k.a. "Uncle Junior" on HBO's

The Sopranos) who first encouraged me to write this. How do I find the words to thank you?

With each new edition of the book, Walter Kaprielian has graciously shared his design expertise.

As an author, I am indebted to public libraries in general—and to reference librarians in particular. They have shown an uncanny ability to track down even the most arcane details in my manuscript. Whenever I travel, it's a special privilege to visit local libraries, autograph my books, and thank the librarians who, day after day, open up the world for us all.

Certainly, no title could exist without strong bookstore support. Booksellers have kept this title on "automatic reorder" since it first appeared in print—and I am grateful.

And to those fine, fine folks at Starbucks who allowed me to linger with my tea, poring over this manuscript for hours on end—well, your good spirits were noted and appreciated.

Finally, I want to thank my son, Seth Rubinstein, who has visited an awesome number of bookstores and libraries with me on behalf of this book. Your unfailing good spirits and terrific attitude have made it all possible. Thank you!

Introduction

❋————————————————————————

I would advise you to read with a pen in your hand . . . for
this will be the best method of imprinting particulars in
your memory.
—Benjamin Franklin

————————————————————————

This book was originally published in 1984 and went into a
second edition in 1992. What's different now—in this second
revised edition?

Well, on the most basic level, I wanted to update the material so it reflects the way we speak today. So, yes, you'll find
fresh examples and updated information throughout the book.
That's for starters.

What's more important, I wanted to revise the book so it
addresses our changing communication needs. Today's speakers face changing audiences, changing formats, and changing
technology. Look through this revised edition, and you'll find
brand-new information on topics that matter much these days:
team presentations, PowerPoint, video clips, creative props,
copyright issues, delivery techniques, military presentations,
and international speeches. The all-new appendix highlights
more than one hundred useful books, Web sites, and professional organizations.

Of course, good communication is never one-sided—and
so this book reflects a dialogue, of sorts. Over the years, I've
written many speeches, coached many speakers, and watched

many presentations. More significantly, I've talked with audiences, and I've listened to their concerns.

Too often, audiences don't get what they want or what they need. Why? Because speakers lack the training that's necessary for success.

It's a rare high school that requires speech proficiency. Colleges and universities grant degrees without requiring public speaking courses. Top MBA programs teach business—but overlook the presentation skills that are needed to succeed in business. Academics and scientists face a "publish or perish" world—but lack the training to turn their dry technical papers into effective presentations. Managers routinely get Power-Point software—but don't have the design skills to use it *well*. (Witness all those presentations filled with endless "word slides"—written in type so small, they could only be read by a low-flying eagle.)

So, we face a supply-and-demand problem. While the demand for good communication is greater than ever, the supply of good communicators is woefully short. Consider this book a clarion call. After all, what could be more important, in any career, than the ability to present ideas?

So, this second revised edition conveys my powerful and passionate belief that *good speeches make a difference.* Good speeches ask questions, pose answers, and get people involved. Good speeches engage our minds and touch our hearts. Good speeches clarify, prod, and inspire—empowering audiences and speakers alike. Good speeches make us stronger. Good speeches make us freer. Above all, good speeches give us a voice. If I have learned anything in my twenty years as a speechwriter and speech coach, it's this: One clear, true voice can, indeed, change things for the better.

I hope this book gives you the clear, true voice to change your own world for the better—one audience at a time.

How to Write & Give a Speech

So You've Been Asked to Give a Speech. Now What?

✳ ───

If you tell them nothing, they go fishing; and if you tell
them something, they go crazy.
—Harry Truman

───

So, you've just been asked to give a speech.

Do you turn to the Internet to do some research? Do you
hunt for some introductory jokes? Do you pull together some
statistics? Not if you're smart.

DETERMINE WHAT YOU WANT TO SAY

Begin, instead, by asking yourself, "What do I *really* want to
say?" Then be ruthless in your answer. You have to focus your
subject. You can't include everything in one speech.

Let me repeat that so it sinks in:

You can't include everything in one speech. In fact, if you
try to include *everything*, your audience will probably come
away with *nothing*. Decide what you really want to say, and
don't throw in any other material.

For example, if you're speaking to a community group
about your corporate ethics, don't think you have to give them
a complete history of your company, too.

If you're speaking to an alumni group to raise funds for

your university, don't throw in a section on the problems of America's high schools.

If you're speaking to the Chamber of Commerce about the need for a new shopping center, don't go off on a tangent about the tax problems of small business.

Get the picture? You're giving a speech, not a dissertation. You can't include every wise thought that's ever crossed your mind.

Remember Voltaire's observation: "The secret of being a bore is to tell everything."

WHAT TO DO IF YOU HAVE NOTHING TO SAY

Suppose—God forbid—that you can't think of anything to talk about? I will give you two anecdotes and two cautions.

> The president of a company called his speechwriter into the room and asked him to write a speech.
> "About what?" the speechwriter asked.
> "Oh," the president said, "about thirty minutes."

Caution: Good speeches do more than fill time. They *say* something.

If you don't know what to say, ask yourself some basic questions about your department, your company, your industry, whatever. Think like a reporter. Dig for good material.

- *Who?*   Who got us into this mess? Who can get us out? Who is really in charge? Who would benefit from this project? Who should get the credit for our success? Who should work on our team? Who will suffer if the merger fails?

- *What?*   What does this situation mean? What actually happened? What went wrong? What is our current status? What do we want to happen? What will the future bring? What is our greatest strength? What is our biggest weakness?

- *Where?*   Where do we go from here? Where can we get help? Where should we cut our budget? Where should we invest? Where should we look for expertise? Where do we want to be in five years? Where can we expand operations? Where will the next problem come from?

- *When?*   When did things start to go wrong? When did things start to improve? When did we first get involved? When will we be ready to handle a new project? When can the company expect to see progress? When will we make money? When will we be able to increase our staff?

- *Why?* Why did this happen? Why did we get involved? Why did we *not* get involved? Why did we get involved so late? Why do we let this mess continue? Why are we holding this meeting? Why should we stick with this course of action? Why should we continue to be patient? Why did they start that program?

- *How?*   How can we get out of this situation? How did we ever get into it? How can we explain our position? How can we protect ourselves? How should we proceed? How should we spend the money? How will we develop our resources? How can we keep our good reputation? How can we improve our image? How does this program really work?

- *What if?*   What if we could change the tax laws? What if we build another plant? What if the zoning regulations don't change? What if we expand into other subsidiaries? What if deregulation backfires? What if costs keep rising?

These questions should lead you to some interesting ideas. Need more inspiration? Pick up a trade paper from another field. Read an academic journal from another discipline. Scan a magazine that represents a different political opinion. Look at a foreign publication. Imagine how the readers of any of these publications would think about your subject.

Or, watch a soap opera you've never seen before. Imagine how the characters portrayed would look at your subject.

In short, take inspiration wherever you can get it. The American painter Grant Wood once admitted, "All the really good ideas I ever had came to me while I was milking a cow."

Also, mystery writer Agatha Christie confessed she got her best ideas while doing the dishes. So, learn to keep your eyes and ears open.

Take your good ideas wherever you get them.

> Albert Einstein, the story goes, was once asked to speak at Harvard. After a splendid introduction, he walked to the podium, looked at the crowd, paused a long time, and said, "I really have nothing to say." Then he sat down.
>
> The audience just sat in stunned silence. Einstein then stood up again and promised, "When I have something to say, I'll come back."

Caution: Unless your name is Albert Einstein, you probably won't get away with this approach.

If you decide you have absolutely nothing to speak about right now, then decline the invitation. Tell the program director you'd be glad to speak at a later date—when you have more information to share. Then, keep your word.

Remember the wisdom of George Eliot: "Blessed is the man who, having nothing to say, abstains from giving in words evidence of the fact."

T W O

Assessing Your Audience

✳

I can never remember being afraid of an audience. If the
audience could do better, they'd be up here on stage and I'd
be out there watching them.
—Ethel Merman

Before you spend one minute researching your topic, before
you write one word of your speech, first analyze your audience.
This chapter will give you a list of important questions to ask.

FAMILIARITY WITH THE SUBJECT

How much does the audience already know about the subject?
Where did they get their information? How much more do they
need or want to know?

ATTITUDES

Why are these people coming to hear you speak? Are they
really interested in the subject, or did someone (perhaps a boss
or a professor) require them to attend? Will they be friendly,
hostile, or apathetic?
    A word of caution about "hostile" audiences: Don't be

too quick to assume an audience will be hostile, and never give a speech with a chip on your shoulder.

Even if the audience doesn't agree with your viewpoint, they might appreciate your open-mindedness, your careful reasoning, and your balanced approach.

A word of advice about apathetic audiences: Some people won't be the least bit interested in your subject. Maybe they're in the audience just because they were obligated to attend, or because it was a chance to get out of the office for a while. Granted, *you* may be interested in your subject, but you'll find plenty of people who aren't.

Surprise them. Startle them. Wake them up. Use anecdotes, examples, and humor to keep their attention.

PRECONCEIVED NOTIONS

Will the audience have preconceived notions about you and your occupation? *Remember:* People are *never* completely objective. Emotion often overrules reason.

Try to imagine how the audience *feels* about you.

One effective way to make an impression on the audience is to shock them a bit—to confront and shatter their preconceptions. If you surprise their emotions, you may influence their reasoning.

For example, if you are a social worker, the audience may have a preconceived notion of you as a bleeding-heart liberal, someone with no idea of what social work costs the taxpayer.

Shatter this preconception. Talk about the need to cut administrative costs in social agencies. Talk about the need for stiffer penalties for those who abuse the system. Talk about the need for professional accountability in the social work profession.

This approach will surprise—and probably impress— them. They will be more likely to *remember* your message.

Appeal to their emotions to influence their thinking.

SIZE

The size of an audience won't affect your subject matter, but it will probably affect your *approach* to the subject matter.

Small groups (say, up to fifteen or twenty people) and large groups have different listening personalities and different psychological orientations. The wise speaker knows how to appeal to the needs of each group.

People in small groups (a board of directors, for example) often know a lot about each other. They can frequently anticipate each other's reactions to new ideas and problems.

People in small groups tend to pay closer attention to you because it's too risky for them to daydream. They may know you, and they may fear being caught off guard by an unexpected question from the podium such as, "I haven't been involved in the administration of these loans, but I'm sure Paul Smith could tell us about that. Paul, would you give us the latest details?"

You can take advantage of this small-group attentiveness by emphasizing reason and by offering solid information.

People in large audiences *don't* normally know everyone else. It's easier for them to sit back and feel anonymous. It's also easier for them to daydream.

Speeches to a large audience can—indeed, often *should*—be more dramatic, more humorous, more emotional. Rhetorical devices that might seem contrived in a small group are now useful. The larger the crowd, the greater the need for "a good show."

People in large audiences tend to think, "Okay, recognize me, entertain me, inspire me. Make me feel good about myself when I leave here."

Cater to these needs.

Also, there's one other important reason to ask about the size—big or small—of an audience.

Obviously, if you assume several hundred people will attend, you may feel embarrassed and disappointed when only forty show up. On the other hand, consider this awful experience: A spokesperson for a health organization frequently spoke to small groups of nurses. One time she showed up at a convention and learned she had to speak to a couple of hundred nurses in a large auditorium. She didn't know how to use the microphone. Her slides weren't bold enough for the new, large space. And she didn't have enough handouts. Is it any wonder she felt overwhelmed and nervous?

AGE

It's important to find out about the *age range* of an audience and to plan your speech accordingly.

What works for one age group might backfire mightily with another. For example, the military successfully uses repetition to tame antsy nineteen-year-olds, but that same training technique might put sixty-year-olds to sleep. (Several military aides once gave a repetitious slide show briefing to President Reagan—only to bring the lights up and find the president sound asleep, along with almost everyone else in the room.)

So, take a moment to think about the ages in your next audience.

Suppose, for example, you must represent your company at a special town meeting. The meeting starts at 7 P.M., and you expect whole families to attend—including parents with young children in tow.

Now, you may *plan* to talk to the homeowners in the audience about the need for new zoning regulations, but you must also be prepared for the pitter-patter of little feet running up and down the aisles and the shrill cries of babies who want to be fed.

Realize that these distractions are inevitable, and that they will probably occur—alas—just when you get to the most critical part of your speech. If you are mentally prepared for these possibilities (and if you have some friendly one-liners ready), you will be less rattled when the disruptions occur.

Or, suppose you're talking to a group of senior citizens. You'll want to pick examples that will reach their particular needs. *Keep in mind:* As people get older, sex-role lines blur, and couples begin sharing more household chores and other responsibilities—including decision-making. So, make sure your presentation involves everyone.

Or, suppose you're talking to a group of college students. Pace your speech to appeal to young people. Be especially careful with humor. *Remember:* People tend to laugh about things they've had some experience with. So, a younger audience may not laugh at the same anecdotes as an older audience. It's simply a lack of "life experience."

MALE/FEMALE RATIO

Ask in advance about the likely male/female ratio, and use this information to help you prepare appropriate statistics and examples.

Be sure to cite appropriate sources as well. If you quote seven experts in your speech, but all seven are male, your oversight will be noticed. Instead, use balanced research that your audience will find credible.

ECONOMIC STATUS

Suppose you speak as a representative of the local electric utility. An affluent, community-minded group might appreciate hearing about your utility's contributions to cultural groups in the area. But people on fixed incomes won't be impressed to learn you give $30,000 each year to the local philharmonic. They would rather hear about specific ways to cut their electric bills or about your utility's efforts to lobby for "energy vouchers" from the government.

Hillary Rodham Clinton learned this lesson the hard way on her twelve-day visit to India, Pakistan, Bangladesh, Nepal, and Sri Lanka in 1995. In the early days of her journey, she touted her husband's accomplishments as president—but unfortunately, her examples proved alien to the poverty-stricken audiences. For example, the first lady mentioned a White House proposal that would take away driver's licenses as punishment for certain offenses—but that meant little to the desperately poor women she spoke to, who had never even ridden in a car.

EDUCATIONAL BACKGROUND

I once heard an engineer who spoke to all sorts of community groups about his corporation's projects. Unfortunately, he spoke the same way to graduate engineering students as he did to retirees who had no previous experience in the field. You can imagine how well his highly technical speeches went over with the retirees.

Of course, you don't need to change the *point* of your speech. Just talk at a level your audience can understand.

POLITICAL ORIENTATION

Has the group taken an official stand on an important national issue? Did the group actively support a local candidate for office? Does the audience take a hard-and-fast view on certain issues?

When Pope John Paul II visited Cuba in 1998, his blunt message of freedom brought applause from the tens of thousands who had gathered for an open-air Mass in Santiago.

CULTURAL LIFE

On a Sunday afternoon, would your audience be more likely to visit a museum or take their kids to an amusement park? Would they read *Popular Mechanics, Forbes,* or *Cosmopolitan*?

All of this information will help you understand your audience. When you understand your audience, you'll give a better speech, and you'll have a much easier time with the question-and-answer session.

But, how can you *get* this information about your audience—and get it quickly? Here are nine tips:

1. *Start by visiting the organization's Web site.* Get background information, so you'll have a good working knowledge of the group prior to any meetings.

2. *Talk with the person who invited you to speak.* If the host is too busy to help, ask for the name and number of someone who can spend more time with you. If possible, talk with this person face-to-face. A telephone conversation is fine, but *don't* settle for a fact sheet from a Web site. A fact sheet won't give you insight into the personality of the audience.

3. *Talk with previous speakers.* See what their experiences were like. What worked? What didn't? What would the speakers do differently if they had a second chance?

4. *Talk with someone who will be in the audience.* What are these meetings usually like? Who was the audience's favorite speaker? Least favorite speaker? Why?

5. *Ask their public relations department.* Can they direct you to information that will give you an idea of the organization's orientation?

6. *Contact the officers of the organization.* But take their information with the proverbial grain of salt. Officers give "official" information, and rarely provide the candid observations you need.

7. *If it's an out-of-town speech, ask the local library for some background or visit the Chamber of Commerce Web site.*

8. *Use common sense.*

9. *Above all, use a little imagination.* Curiosity will bring its own rewards. As Einstein advised, "The important thing is not to stop questioning. Curiosity has its own reason for existing."

AN ADDITIONAL WORD TO THE WISE

It's not smart to give the same speech to different audiences. Why?

• You will eventually get tired of presenting the same material, and your boredom will show.

• No two audiences are alike. Your listeners will have different attitudes, special interests, and pet peeves. A direct proportion exists here: The more you try to lump all of your audiences together, the more they will disregard—and even dislike—you.

• You never know if someone in the audience might have heard you give the identical speech somewhere else.

Improbable? Think about this embarrassing situation. One Monday morning at the Waldorf-Astoria, a minister pronounced the benediction before a breakfast meeting of the American Newspaper Publishers Association.

Later in the day, he returned to the Waldorf-Astoria to give the blessing at an Associated Press luncheon. It was—you guessed it—the same prayer, and listeners who attended both meetings were quick to pick up the repeated phrases.

Even worse, the *New York Times* was quick to pick up the story, and ran it under the headline "Invoking the Familiar."

Funny? Sure—as long as it happened to someone else and not to you.

THREE

Where and When Will You Speak?

✳ ────────────────────────────────────

I like people who refuse to speak until they are ready to speak.
—Lillian Hellman

───────────────────────────────────────

After you've determined what your audience will be like, the next step (yes, you should do this before you head to the Internet and before you put pen to paper) is to consider where and when you will give your speech.

WHERE

Let's start with the basics. Where, *exactly*, will you give the speech?

- In the training center of a large corporation?
- In a university auditorium?
- In a high school classroom?
- In a hotel conference room?
- In a gymnasium?

- In a restaurant?
- On an outdoor platform?

Does it make any difference? Yes.

Plan a Speech That's Appropriate to the Setting

For example:

- If you're speaking on an outdoor platform (as is common at graduations), be sensitive to the weather. Know how to "wrap up" your speech in a hurry if a June thunderstorm cuts you short.

- If you must speak in a large banquet hall, have some one-liners ready for the inevitable moments when waiters interrupt your speech to serve coffee and drown out your words with the clatter of dishes.

- If you'll be in a hotel conference room, bring along some signs reading, "Quiet please—Meeting in progress." Post these signs on the doors to alert people passing through the corridor.

If you've never seen the location, ask the program host for a rough sketch of the room. How big is the area? Where will you stand? Where will the audience sit? Are the chairs movable? "Seeing" all this on paper first will help you feel more comfortable when you actually speak there.

You might be able to tie the setting into the theme of your speech. Consider this opening by Gerald Greenwald, vice chairman of Chrysler, to the Society of Automotive Engineers banquet in Detroit:

> This is also the first time in my life that I've given a speech atop a lazy Susan! Leave it to engineers, in the city of wheels, to put *the speaker* on a wheel!

To garner media attention, you can choose a location that will generate publicity. For example, when Mars, Inc., announced a much ballyhooed color addition to its beloved M&M chocolate candies, they unveiled the new blue M&M at the Empire State Building—which was duly lighted in blue for the occasion.

WHEN

Again, the basics. When, *exactly*, will you give the speech?

- At a breakfast meeting?
- At a mid-morning seminar?
- Just before lunch?
- During lunch?
- After lunch, before people return to work?
- As part of a mid-afternoon panel?
- At 4 P.M., as the final speaker in the day's seminar?
- At 9 P.M., as the after-dinner speaker?
- At 11 P.M., as the last in a string of after-dinner speakers?

Plan a Speech That Suits the Time of Day

Use your imagination. Always look at the event from the audience's perspective. What will be on *their* minds?

For example:

- You must be especially brief and succinct at a breakfast meeting. Why? Because your breakfast meeting forced the audience to get up an hour or two early. And because they still face a whole day's work ahead of them. If your speech is not organized and clear and concise—and if they can't get to their offices on time—they will resent you.

• If you speak on a mid-afternoon panel, find out whether you'll speak first or last. Panel presentations run notoriously behind schedule, and the last speaker often feels "squeezed" for time. Be realistic, and be prepared to give a shortened presentation, if necessary.

• If you speak after a banquet (perhaps to celebrate a retirement), know that the audience has been eating and drinking for several hours. They will be in a good mood. They will want to *stay* in a good mood. Don't ruin their evening with an overly long, overly serious speech. Adlai Stevenson got it right when he said, "The best after-dinner speech I ever heard was, 'Waiter, I'll take the check.'"

Should You Request a Particular Time Slot?

Yes, if it will improve the effect of your speech.

Suppose, for example, you learn that you're scheduled to speak after a series of award presentations. You suspect, and rightly so, that the audience will be restless after hearing all those thank-you speeches. What should you do?

Be assertive. Let the program host know that you're willing to listen to the award presentations, but that you're not willing to follow them.

If you are showing overheads or PowerPoint and will require a darkened room, ask to speak mid-morning. Avoid darkened rooms immediately after lunch or dinner. They are conducive to sleep—and the last thing you want is to have your speech interrupted by snores.

A Caution About Out-of-Town Conferences

Know what you're up against. People who travel to a conference in sunny Florida in the middle of January aren't going there just to hear your speech. People who go to a conference in Las Vegas may not even want to hear your speech at all.

Consider Hubert H. Humphrey's advice for addressing restless audiences:

> You say, "Buzz-buzz-buzz-buzz-buzz—Franklin Delano Roosevelt! Buzz-buzz-buzz-buzz-buzz—Harry S. Truman! Buzz-buzz-buzz-buzz-buzz—John Fitzgerald Kennedy!" And then you get the hell out of there before they start throwing rolls at each other.

How to Research a Speech

❋ ───────────────────────────────

We cannot have expression till there is something to be
expressed.
—Margaret Fuller

───────────────────────────────

Now that you've determined the nature of your audience and
considered where and when you will speak, the next step is to
gather information for your speech. But don't rush off to the
library yet. Instead, just sit down and *think*.

USE YOUR HEAD

Your best information source is always *your own head*. Ask
yourself, "What do I *already* know about this subject?" Then
jot down your thoughts.

Don't worry about organization at this point. Just make
some rough notes. Write down important facts, opinions,
examples—whatever information you already know. Let your
notes sit for a day or two, if possible. Then review them.

Now, begin to look for *specific* information in the form of
statistics, quotations, examples, definitions, comparisons, and
contrasts.

If you don't have enough specifics or enough *variety* of

specifics, do some research and get them. Again, start your research close to home and branch out as needed:

- Visit relevant Web sites.

- Leaf through magazines related to the subject.

- Consult with friends and business associates.

- Call up a specialist in the field and ask for a comment.

- Introduce yourself to a reference librarian, explain your speech assignment, and ask for resources.

MAKE GOOD USE OF THE LIBRARY

Reference librarians are invaluable to any speechwriter. Absolutely invaluable. They know their way around a library and can save you countless hours of time and frustration.

Many reference librarians even handle inquiries over the telephone. If this service is available at your local library, keep the telephone number handy.

If you expect to give many speeches during your career, become friendly with a reference librarian. Take a reference librarian to lunch. It's a worthwhile investment in your career.

Another worthwhile investment? Become familiar with some basic reference books and Web sites. I've included a list of references at the end of this book. They will help you write better speeches—and they will help you do it faster.

Internet access will bring you a wealth of information, but if you write a lot of speeches you will also want to buy some good reference books for your personal library.

WHAT TO LEAVE OUT

As the speaker, you're in control: *You* get to choose the precise topic. You also get to decide what information stays and what information goes. What *not* to say is just as important as what *to* say.

Leave out:

* irrelevant details

* boring details

* any information you can't verify

* anything you wouldn't want to see quoted in print the next day

* anything you wouldn't want to be reminded of next year.

APPROACH THE TOPIC FROM THE AUDIENCE'S PERSPECTIVE

Your audience can understand your subject only by relating it to their own ideas and problems and experiences. So, approach the subject from *their* perspective, not *your* perspective.

For example, don't just complain about your industry's problems. Even if you have some legitimate complaints, your audience will probably not care. They have enough problems of their own.

Instead, relate *your* concerns to *their* concerns. Find the emotional "hook" that will help the audience understand your message.

Talk about audience *benefits*. Show how the audience would benefit if your industry could solve its problems. Would the audience save money? Save time? Be healthier? Be happier?

Approach the topic from their perspective, and you'll be more effective. It's a fact: Audiences tend to trust—and to like—speakers who show a real understanding of them.

HOW TO USE STATISTICS FOR IMPACT

Some people think statistics are boring. These people have not heard the right statistics.

Statistics can be downright interesting, *if* you:

1. *Make the statistics seem real to your audience.* Try, "While we're sitting here for an hour and debating the value of sex education in the schools, 'x number' of teenage girls will give birth to illegitimate children."

   Or, "While you're watching your favorite TV show tonight, forty-five people will call the national cocaine hot line to ask for help. Could one of them be *your* child?"

2. *Explain what your statistics mean.* Jim Press, COO of Toyota and chairman of the auto industry's major trade group (Alliance of Automobile Manufacturers), made statistics come alive when he spoke at the opening of the New York Auto Show in 2001.

   "We've not only been experiencing record sales, but there's also a renewed passion about cars: America's love affair with the automobile still remains the source of our strength.

   "How do I know this?

   "*Adweek* magazine surveyed Americans about their cars and came up with these notable statistics:

• More than half the men and almost half the women surveyed actually 'talk' to their cars . . . now, I don't know if that's on a daily basis, but we all know good communication is the key to a solid relationship.

• And one out of every four people surveyed actually think of their car as a 'member of the family.'

   "Ladies and Gentlemen: I ask you . . . what other product does that in American life?"

3. *Put statistics in simple terms.* Don't just say that your senator will mail "x" million items to his constituents this year. Instead, explain that this amounts to about three deliveries to every mailbox in his district. Everyone who has a mailbox can relate to that statistic.

4. *Round off the numbers.* Say "almost one million customers," not "997,755 customers." Make it easy for the audience to *hear and remember* your statistics.

   Here's how Sam Nunn, former U.S. senator and CEO of the Nuclear Threat Initiative, addressed the threat posed by nuclear weapons—in a speech given less than six months prior to the terrorist attacks of 9/11: "More than 1,000 tons of highly enriched uranium, and at least 150 tons of weapons-grade plutonium, exist in the Russian weapons complex—enough to build at least 60,000 nuclear weapons. And terrorist groups and rogue states are trying to exploit the situation."

5. *Use numbers sparingly.* Audiences cannot absorb more than a couple of numbers at a time. If you use too many statistics, you will lose your listeners.

6. *Be graphic.* Try to paint a picture with numbers. Say, "It's as long as four football fields." Or, "The stack of papers would be as tall as the bank building across the street." Or, "You'd have to dig a hole big enough to hide a supertanker."

   My point is: Let your audience *see* your numbers by using real-life examples.

   Listen to an excerpt of a speech by FBI Director William Sessions to the Commonwealth Club of California. "Just how much is a hundred pounds of heroin? Well, let me describe it this way: Even just twenty-five pounds of high-quality heroin is enough to overdose every man, woman, and child in the city of San Francisco."

   Now, that statement is really graphic.

7. *Do not apologize for using statistics.* Inexperienced speakers often say, "I hate to bore you with statistics, *but . . .*" After this apology, they proceed to bore their audiences with poorly chosen and poorly used statistics.

Avoid this pitfall. If you follow the guidelines in this chapter, your statistics will *not* be boring. They will, in fact, add a lot of interest to your speech.

HOW TO USE QUOTATIONS

> Next to the originator of a good sentence is the first quoter of it.
> —Ralph Waldo Emerson

Audiences love quotations, *if* you:

1. *Use some variety.* If you're speaking about productivity, for example, don't just quote the U.S. Department of Labor. Use a variety of sources. Try:

- Abraham Lincoln ("My father taught me to work; he did not teach me to love it.")

- Robert Frost ("The world is full of willing people; some willing to work, the rest willing to let them.")

- The Bible ("The harvest truly is plenteous, but the labourers are few.")

- The president of a local union

- The manager of a large personnel department

- An industrial psychologist

- An anonymous commentator ("People come up to me and say, 'Yours is the best-run factory in the United States.' And that makes me feel great. But I know our productivity will start to decline if we ever become too proud or too careless.")

2. *Avoid lengthy or complicated quotations.* Keep quotations short. Cut or paraphrase any "slow parts."

3. *Blend the quotation into the text.* Never say, "quote . . . unquote." Instead, pause a moment and let your voice emphasize the quotation.

4. *Appear comfortable with the quotation.* Never quote anybody unless you're sure you can pronounce the name right. I once heard a speaker quote "the well-known German writer, Goethe." Unfortunately, he pronounced the name as "Goath"—and the quotation just fell flat.

5. *Use quotations judiciously.* A speech should reflect *your* thoughts and expertise, so don't quote dozens of other people. In a fifteen-minute speech, you can probably use two or three quotations. *Remember:* The impact of your quotations will decline sharply as their number grows.

HOW TO USE DEFINITIONS

What do you mean when you speak about "liquidity problems"? About "decreasing profit margins"? About "a captive finance company"?

1. *Define your terms in everyday words.* Avoid "dictionary" definitions. "According to Webster, . . ." is a phrase that sounds feeble and amateurish.

2. *Try a definition with a light touch.* You might want to ask a six-year-old for a definition of "management compensation." You'll get some amusing definitions that could add interest to your speech.

3. *Reinforce your definition with vivid details.* Here's how Tom Daschle, Senate majority leader from South Dakota, defined the leadership role of the United States: "We are the only nation on the earth able to project power in every region of the earth. Consider this: B-2s stationed in Missouri flew halfway around the world to help bring an end to the ethnic cleansing in Kosovo and returned home without stopping to land."

HOW TO USE COMPARISONS AND CONTRASTS

Use everyday comparisons to which people can easily relate.

When Leo Durocher was manager of the Brooklyn Dodgers, he was booed for pulling a pitcher out late in a close game. Afterward, a reporter asked him how he felt about the crowd's reaction. Durocher's comparison? "Baseball is like church. Many attend. Few understand."

Rudolph Giuliani compared the World Trade Center to a great battlefield in his farewell address as mayor of New York City. Speaking adjacent to the rubble at Ground Zero, Guiliani said, "This is going to be a place that is remembered one hundred and one thousand years from now, like the great battlefields of Europe and of the United States—Normandy or Valley Forge or Bunker Hill or Gettysburg."

HOW TO USE EXAMPLES

Specific examples will help your message "stick" in the audience's mind. Donald Rumsfeld, secretary of defense for the United States, addressed the 2001 NATO North Atlantic Council in Belgium by citing Dick Cheney as an example: [When] "Vice President Cheney appeared before the U.S. Senate for his confirmation hearings as Secretary of Defense—not one person uttered the word 'Iraq.' Within a year, he was preparing for war in the Persian Gulf."

In an address to the nation on stem cell research, President George W. Bush used the power of personal examples: "I have friends whose children suffer from juvenile diabetes. Nancy Reagan has written me about President Reagan's struggle with Alzheimer's. My own family has confronted the tragedy of childhood leukemia."

HOW TO USE ANECDOTES

Audiences love good anecdotes. Even more important, they love the speakers who tell them.

The appendix of this book lists many books and Web sites where you can find great anecdotes. But you don't need to spend hours on the Internet or in a library. Some of the best research details will spring from your own experience.

"The Great Communicator," Ronald Reagan, certainly knew the power of a good anecdote. Here's a brief personal story he shared with the National Association of Evangelicals:

> During World War II, I remember a rally to promote war bonds was held at Madison Square Garden in New York. The rally featured great figures from government and big names from Hollywood, but it was a $54-a-month buck private who spoke nine words that no one there will ever forget. His name was Joe Louis. He walked to center stage and said: "I know we'll win, because we're on God's side." There was a moment's silence, then the cheering nearly took the roof off.

Norman Mineta, U.S. secretary of transportation, drew on his own painful experiences as an American of Japanese ancestry when he spoke at the University of Rochester just weeks after the 9/11 attack on America. Mineta described the terrible treatment of Japanese-Americans during World War II—and urged people not to mistreat Arab and Muslim Americans in

Writing the Speech

❋ ────────────────────────────────

Planning to write is not writing. Outlining . . .
researching . . . talking to people about what you're
doing . . . none of that is writing. Writing is writing.
—E. L. Doctorow

────────────────────────────────────

All right. Enough thinking, enough planning, enough researching. Now's the time to sit down and write.

What do you have to do to write a good speech? Two things:

1. Make it simple.
2. Make it short.

What do you have to do to write a *great* speech?

1. Make it simpler.
2. Make it shorter.

In this chapter, I'll tell you how to make your speech simple and easy to understand. In the next chapter, I'll show you
specific techniques to make it short—and memorable.

These two chapters are the guts of the book. Read them
carefully. Reread them with a pencil in your hand. Mark the
hell out of them. Because they tell you everything this professional speechwriter knows about writing speeches.

the wake of the terrorist attacks. Mineta's personal sto
strengthened his political message.

SOME FINAL THOUGHTS ABOUT RESEA

Sophisticated listeners will question the source of yo
mation. Make sure the source is *reputable* and *approp
your particular audience.

Also, be sure to use a *mixture* of material in your s
maybe one or two quotations, an example, a couple of
tistics, and a comparison. This variety will make you
more interesting and more credible.

Be aware: Some people just don't assimilate cert
of information. "Numbers people" may consider a
"frivolous" or "invalid." "People people" may mistru
tics, preferring to receive their information in anecdo

Use a combination of techniques to get your
across.

As Bette Midler describes the way she puts to
effective show, "I always try to balance the light
heavy—a few tears for the human spirit in with the se
the fringes." That same balance can work to the adv
anyone trying to gather research for a speech. The v
prove powerful—and create a more memorable spee

THE NEVER-FAIL FORMULA

Here's the formula for a successful speech. It works every time.

- Tell them what you're going to tell them.
- Tell them.
- Tell them what you've told them.

TELL THEM WHAT YOU'RE GOING TO TELL THEM: THE OPENING

I won't mince words. The opening is the toughest part. If you don't hook your listeners within the first thirty seconds, your cause is probably lost.

Start with a "grabber"—an anecdote, a startling statistic, a quotation, a personal observation, a literary, historical, or biblical allusion. Use whatever it takes to get the audience's attention. Give them a good taste of what's to come.

It can be risky to begin a speech with a joke. If it falls flat, you're off to a terrible start, so don't use a joke unless you are *absolutely* sure you can deliver it well. Even then, use a joke only if it's short and if it relates to the topic of the speech.

Never, *never*, open by saying something like, "I heard a really funny story today. It doesn't have anything to do with my speech, but at least it'll give you a good laugh."

Instead, try one of these opening techniques:

Praise the Audience

Denny Clements, group vice president/GM, Lexus Division, opened his speech to the Iowa Better Business Bureau in Des Moines with this praise:

Integrity is woven into the very fabric of Iowa, its history, and its people. Family, faith, and education have always come first.

I was not surprised to find out that Iowa State University was chartered less than a year after you achieved statehood. Nor was I surprised to find out that the Underground Railroad was very active here during the Civil War. I was not surprised to find out that the intrepid Wright Brothers were Iowans.

I *was* a little surprised to find out you have *snow skiing* . . . you know, it takes a people with considerable imagination, vision, and determination to look at the plains of Iowa and say, "Let's build a ski resort."

Iowa has provided our country with a president, two first ladies, and John Wayne, who will forever be an American symbol of strength, character, and integrity. I'm proud to be here, and Lexus is proud to conduct business here.

Make a Reference to the Date

Giving a speech on June 14? Find out what happened on that date in history and see if it connects to the theme of your speech. The "date in history" technique is catchy, clever, and irresistibly quotable to the press. Even better, it's quick and easy to prepare.

The appendix at the back of this book gives detailed listings about Web sites and reference books that tell "what happened on this date in history." You'll want to bookmark these resources.

Ask Some Questions

Questions are an effective way to involve an audience. Listen to this opener by Fred Halperin, chairman of the International Association of Business Communicators Research Foundation:

Let me start by asking you a few questions. How many of you would say that you practice excellent communication for your organization?

Now, let's say your communications department costs your organization $100,000 a year. What kind of return on investment would you say your department gives your organization? One hundred percent would be $100,000; that means your value pays for your cost. Would it be less than a hundred percent? More?

Okay, now how would your CEO answer that question?

Use Local Details

When Bill Dahlberg, CEO of the Southern Company, spoke to the DeKalb (Georgia) Chamber of Commerce, he opened with this local connection:

> This is sort of like coming home. . . . Fifty years ago, my father moved our family to a little unincorporated community, just southwest of Stone Mountain, called Mountainview. The biggest thing there was Hiram Crow's store. If you went down the road another quarter of a mile, you'd come to Louis Crow's store. If you went a little bit further down the road, you'd come to Jay Crow's Dairy and Store. It may have been the first Mom-and-Pop chain in all of DeKalb County.
>
> My first three years in school were spent in a two-room schoolhouse. I believe we had a coal stove for heat. I do know the bathrooms were outside.
>
> DeKalb County now, of course, has huge schools—huge, overcrowded schools—schools with trailers in back. Air-conditioned trailers, I might add.

Cite Your Professional Credentials—or Your Personal Credentials—or, Even Better, Both

E. James Morton, CEO of John Hancock Mutual Life Insurance Company, spoke to the National Conference on Work and Family Issues and created a strong rapport with this opening:

> Well, my instructions were to be as provocative and visionary as I can. . . . I am, by training, an actuary. A common definition is that an actuary is someone who didn't have enough personality to be an accountant. Provocativeness and vision are not normally in our bag of

tricks. But, we do know a little bit about demographics and how to project trends, so let me do the best I can per instructions.

I might also add, on a personal basis, that my own situation does give me a fairly broad range of experience in family matters.

I have a ninety-year-old mother; three daughters whose ages are forty-one, twenty-six, and eight; a nine-month-old grandson; and a baby-boomer wife whose mother is a World War II Icelandic war bride, and who lives in another city to which I commute on weekends.

So I believe that I can relate closely to practically any demographic or family situation that anyone can bring up.

Openings for Special Circumstances

If you're making a return engagement

Let the audience know how pleased you are to address them again.

Donald Coonley, chief national bank examiner, took this lighthearted approach when he addressed the Urban Bankers Forum:

> To be invited twice to speak to the same group is a great honor. A return performance is not always automatic. And Winston Churchill once used this fact to his advantage.
>
> Churchill received an invitation from George Bernard Shaw to one of his opening plays back in the early 1900s. Shaw's note read: "Enclosed are two tickets to the first-night performance of a play of mine. Bring a friend—if you have one."
>
> Not to be outdone, Churchill shot back this reply: "Dear G.B.S., I thank you very much for the invitation and the tickets. Unfortunately, I am engaged on that night, but could I have tickets for the second performance—if there is one?"
>
> I am happy and honored that there is—for me—a second performance before this group.

If you are a substitute speaker

So, you're a last-minute invitee? Get it out in the open, and move on. Don't belabor the fact.

Yes, they may have been expecting someone else, but if you're interesting, they'll be very glad to hear *you*. Really.

If you are speaking out of town
Avoid this all-too-common opening, "It's great being here in Cincinnati/Philadelphia/Walla Walla."

The first thing your audience wants to know is "Why?" "Why on earth," they're saying to themselves, "are you so thrilled to be here in Cincinnati/Philadelphia/Walla Walla?"

Were you born here? Did you go to college here? Did you start your first job here? If so, then *tell* the audience. They'll appreciate the personal connection.

If you're the last to speak
Keep it brief, and make it lively. *Remember:* The poor audience has been sitting there listening to speech after speech—each probably more tedious than the one before! So, give them a break, and let them end on an upbeat.

One time, George Bernard Shaw had to follow a series of speakers, and he took this approach: After he was introduced and the applause subsided, he simply said, "Ladies and gentlemen: The subject may not be exhausted, but we are." With that summation, he sat down.

There might be a lesson in that.

Some Cautions About Beginning a Speech

It's not necessary—or even desirable—to begin with, "Good evening, ladies and gentlemen." Greetings like this are really just fillers. Skip them. Jump right in with the first line of your speech.

The same goes with most introductory *thank you*'s. They can sound pretty feeble, and feeble is not the way to begin a speech. Whatever you do, avoid trite openings. Almost every run-of-the-mill (read: boring) speech begins with something like, "It's such a wonderful pleasure to be here today." Who is this speaker trying to kid? Since when is speechmaking such a pleasure?

Everyone knows that giving a speech is hard work. Most people would rather do *anything* than stand up and give a speech.

Don't flash a phony smile and open with a glib line. Audiences are quick to spot insincerity—and they're slow to forgive you for it.

If you're really enthusiastic about giving your speech, it will show in your content and delivery. You won't have to fake it with flowery openings.

TELL THEM: THE BODY

> Organize is what you do before you do something, so that when you do it, it's not all mixed up.
> —Christopher Robin in A. A. Milne's *Winnie the Pooh*

Inexperienced speechwriters want to say everything, and that's where they make their first mistake. Focus your material, and limit the number of points you make. If you concentrate on one central idea, your audience will stand a better chance of understanding you.

Wait a minute. Are you saying to yourself, "But my topic is so important, I've *got* to get everything across"?

Don't get carried away with your own importance.

If you try to say *everything*, your audience will come away with *nothing*. It's as simple as that.

No matter what your speech is about, you must limit, focus, and organize your material. There are lots of ways to do this. Use whatever method works best for you.

Chronological Order

Try dividing your material into time units—from past to present to future—or whatever pattern seems to fit. This method can be effective because it *connects* everything.

Show how historical changes affect the quality of people's lives. If possible, show how these changes affect the quality of your *audience*'s lives.

Cause and Effect

Did you start an employee program that has produced positive benefits throughout the company? Then show why it's so successful.

Did something go wrong with your marketing plan and cause problems elsewhere? Use that cause-and-effect relationship to organize your speech.

Was your transportation section able to reduce its gasoline costs this year? Tell what caused that improvement: better maintenance, more efficient routes, etc.

Numerical Order

You can go from the highest to the lowest number, or from the lowest to the highest.

Suppose you want to show how your volume of oil production has increased. Look at the numbers as part of an escalating trend. Relate them to specific events so the audience can see *why* your oil production went up.

Suppose you want to show how theft has been reduced in your distribution department. Explain to your audience *why* those numbers went down.

Always relate numbers to *human* events. That's the only way they will make sense to your audience—which will, presumably, be composed largely of humans.

Problem-Solution Approach

Is there something wrong with your tuition aid program? Then tell your audience about the problem and propose some solutions.

Do this with candor and honesty. If you have a problem, bring it out into the open. Chances are, your audience *already* knows about the problem. Admit it honestly, and you'll come across as credible.

Also, if you think your proposed solutions will be difficult, say so. No one likes a snow job.

Geographical Order

Organizing a national sales conference? Start by reporting sales in the eastern districts and work west.

Reviewing the physical expenditures of your company's plants? Start with the northern ones and work south.

Evaluating the productivity of your bank's branches? Take it neighborhood by neighborhood.

Alphabetical Order

Why not? This certainly is easy for the audience to follow. And there are times when alphabetical order may be the only way to organize your information—lists of committees or departments, for cxample.

Psychological Order

Sometimes it's best to organize your speech based on the psychological needs of the audience.

What will they find most acceptable? Most important? Most interesting? Put that first.

Think about the attitudes your audience may have. If you expect them to be hostile or resistant, then ease slowly into your speech. Begin on common ground and put your most acceptable ideas up front. Don't expect to convince everyone of everything. There's usually a limit to the controversial ideas that any audience can accept.

Some sensitive areas in the business world (pro/antinuclear power and labor/management confrontations, for example) *require* attention to psychological order.

Transitions

No matter which method you use, make sure you follow the order *smoothly*. Do not get sidetracked. If you say something like, "But before I do that, I'd like to give you a little background on the history of our firm," you're heading for trouble.

Keep things moving. Use strong transitions to help the audience follow your ideas. Try such transitional phrases as:

* Moving on to the second territory . . .

* Now let's take a look at . . .

* So much for supply, but what about demand?

* Switching now to the western division . . .

* Looking ahead to the next five years . . .

Special Circumstances

How to handle a crisis

Your company faces a serious crisis, and it's your job to explain the issue to the employees.

1. Present several undeniable facts that show the seriousness of the situation. Do this *up front*. Be sure to do it

without exaggeration, or the audience will suspect your motives.

2. Explore possible solutions to the crisis: tighter budget control, increased productivity, etc.

3. Solicit the ideas and support of *everyone* in the company to make the program work. Let them know exactly what you expect from them.

Caution: Don't treat every situation like a crisis, or you will lose credibility. You are entitled to one, maybe two, crises in your career. No more.

If you try to turn every situation into a crisis, your audience will see you as the little boy (or girl) who cried wolf once too often. They won't bother to listen anymore.

How to admit you've made a mistake

Have you shown an error in judgment? Made a foolish decision? Chosen the wrong person for a job? Backed the losing team? Pursued a dangerous course?

No sense in hiding your role. Everyone already knows. So, bring your mistake out in the open, clear the air, and set the stage to move on.

Listen to the way President Reagan addressed the nation on the Iran-Contra affair:

> Now what should happen when you make a mistake is this: You take your knocks, you learn your lessons, and then you move on. That's the healthiest way to deal with a problem. . . .
>
> You know, by the time you reach my age, you've made plenty of mistakes, and if you've lived your life properly, you learn. You put things in perspective. You pull your energies together. You change. You go forward.
>
> My fellow Americans, I have a great deal that I want to accomplish with you and for you over the next two years, and, the Lord willing, that's exactly what I intend to do. Good night and God bless you.

How to handle an emotional moment

Trying to deal with a tragedy? A community crisis? A painful situation? Be realistic. Your emotions may overcome you, so it's wise to think about how you might handle yourself *before* you begin your speech.

Perhaps this real-life example will prove both inspirational and instructional: When President George Bush paid tribute to the forty-seven dead crew members of the battleship *Iowa*, he said, "They came from Hidalgo, Texas, and Cleveland, Ohio; from Tampa, Florida, and Costa Mesa, California. They came to the Navy as strangers, served the Navy as shipmates and friends, and left the Navy as brothers in eternity."

An audience of three thousand mourners listened as the president's words soon gave way to emotion. His voice cracked when he said, "Your men are under a different command now, one that knows no rank, only love; knows no danger, only peace." Then, tears filled President Bush's eyes.

Apparently, the president feared he would lose control of his emotions, so he wisely dropped the final lines of his address, managed to say, "May God bless them," swallowed hard, turned abruptly, and left the lectern.

Later on, both President and Mrs. Bush walked among the aisles of mourners, comforting them and embracing them. During difficult moments, Mrs. Bush wept openly. President Bush managed to keep his tears in check—but he prudently kept a handkerchief in his hand, just in case he needed it.

How to express disappointment

Suppose some big plan failed—and failed publicly. Now it's your responsibility to tell the audience why the old plan failed and to make some new proposals.

Beware. The audience may be extremely sensitive about the issue and they may fear being blamed for the whole mess.

Reassure them that the original plan was a good one. Say it made sense based on the information available at the time it was conceived. Say no one could have predicted the sudden changes in events that caused the original plan to fail.

Once the audience feels safe from any finger-pointing, they will be receptive to your message.

State the problem clearly and objectively. Admit disappointment, but don't dwell on past failures. Let your emphasis be on a new plan that's based on new data.

How to turn a negative into a positive

Did your fund-raising campaign fail to meet its goals? Then find a way to turn those negative facts into a positive truth.

As Frank Lloyd Wright put it, "The truth is more important than the facts." If some of your facts are disappointing, try to find a larger, more positive truth.

One Final Point

Double-check your speech to make sure that if you say "first," you follow it with a "second." Otherwise your audience—and maybe even you—will become hopelessly lost.

Be careful, though, not to overuse the "first, second, third" references. They can be confusing.

TELL THEM WHAT YOU TOLD THEM: THE CONCLUSION

Now's the time to sum it up—simply and directly. No new thoughts, please. You must avoid the temptation to "stick in" any additional points at the end. It's too late for that.

Your conclusion may be the only thing the audience remembers, so make it memorable.

Here are some effective ways to end a speech:

Use Compelling Imagery

Here's how Thomas Kuhn, president of the Edison Electric Institute, wrapped up his speech at EEI's annual conference:

Energy, efficiency, and ingenuity. They are the hope for the future, just as surely as they are the foundation of the past. This is our story. It is a story of progress and growth, a story we must tell others.

The road we travel is a long one; it stretches all the way back from the present to that first energy-using ancestor, and on ahead to the far horizon. I don't know what's beyond that horizon, but I'll bet on this: We will meet it head-on, with a fire in our bellies, a wind in our sails, steam up, and a full charge!

Share Your Personal Philosophy

When Harvey Mackay, bestselling author of *Swim with the Sharks Without Being Eaten Alive*, gave the MBA commencement address at Penn State University, he created a strong emotional appeal by sharing this story from his boyhood:

When I was a kid, my father knew a guy named Bernie who had started out his career with a vegetable stand, worked hard all his life, and eventually became wealthy as a fruit and vegetable wholesaler.

Every summer, when the first good watermelons came in, Dad would take me down to Bernie's warehouse and we'd have a feast. Bernie would choose a couple of watermelons just in from the field, crack them open, and hand each of us a big piece. Then, with Bernie taking the lead, we'd eat only the heart of the watermelon—the reddest, juiciest, most perfect part—and throw the rest away.

My father never made a lot of money. We were raised to clean our plates and not waste food. Bernie was my father's idea of a rich man. I always thought it was because he'd been such a success in business.

It was years before I realized my father admired Bernie's "richness" because he knew how to stop work in the middle of a summer day, sit down with his friends, and spend time eating the heart of the watermelon.

Being rich isn't about money. Being rich is a state of mind. Some of us, no matter how much money we have, will never be free enough to take the time to stop and eat the heart of the watermelon. And some of us will be rich without ever being more than a paycheck ahead of the game. . . .

From my standpoint, that's what it's all about. . . .

Never stop learning.
Believe in yourself, even when no one else does.
Find a way to make a difference, and . . .
Eat the heart of the watermelon.
Then go out and make your own tracks in the snow.

Tie Your Theme to an Anniversary

Vice President Dan Quayle once addressed the American Bar Association on the need for reform in America's legal system—a topic, one might suppose, that would ruffle more than a few feathers at an ABA convention.

Quayle hit his audience with a series of unsettling rhetorical questions, "Does America really need seventy percent of the world's lawyers? Is it healthy for our economy to have eighteen million new lawsuits coursing through the system annually?"

Then, he concluded by tying his criticisms to a significant anniversary:

> On this bicentennial of the Bill of Rights, we should remind ourselves of the memorable words of Justice Robert Jackson:
> "Civil liberties had their origin, and must find their ultimate guaranty, in the faith of the people."
> Our job in government, and your job as leaders in the law, is to strengthen the faith of the people—in the resolute protection of their rights, and in the effective delivery of justice.

Tell a Humorous Story to Illustrate Your Point

When Mitchell Daniels Jr., vice president of corporate affairs for Eli Lilly, spoke at a University of Indianapolis commencement, he sent out the graduates chuckling over this bit of humor:

> I will close with a story, and with sincere congratulations. . . .
> The story is a favorite of President Reagan's, and concerns the

businessman who ordered a floral bouquet sent to the grand opening of a friend's new branch office. He arrived at the ceremony and found to his dismay that his flowers had been delivered with a card that said, "Rest in Peace."

The next day, he called the florist and irately demanded a refund, only to be told, "Don't worry, just think of it this way. Somewhere in town yesterday some poor soul was buried under a sign that said, "Good luck in your new location."

That's what I wish you now—good luck in all your new locations.

End with a Strong Rhetorical Question

Something like this can be effective, "Can we afford to do it? A more relevant question is, can we afford *not* to?"

End with Words That *Sound* Strong

- "We need to return to that old-fashioned notion of competition—where *substance*, not *subsidies*, determines the winner." This ending focuses the audience's attention on two contrasting words that begin with the same syllable—*sub*.

- "We worked hard to get this department in tip-top shape. We plan to keep it that way." *Tip-top* repeats the opening and closing consonant sounds.

- "Yes, we ran into some problems, but we corrected them. Perhaps our message should be 'Sighted sub, sank same.'" Good use of alliteration—repetition of initial consonant sounds.

- "Our personnel department's training program works on the premise that 'earning' naturally follows 'learning.'" Rhyme can be catchy, but use it judiciously.

End with a Strong Commitment

At the National Day of Prayer and Remembrance following the 9/11 terrorist attacks, Vice Admiral Thad Allen, U.S. Coast Guard, concluded his remarks at Norfolk Waterside Park this way:

> We cannot explain the unexplainable. We cannot change the past. We cannot restore what is lost.
> But we can be here, and we can say to those who are suffering: We believe . . .
> We live by our core values of honor, respect and devotion to duty. We *honor* those who died. We *respect* our law and authorities. We remain *devoted to duty* whatever that duty is, and wherever that duty may take us.
> We will be Semper Paratus . . . Always Ready.

How to Make It Simple

❋ ───────────────────────────────────

The most valuable of all talents is that of never using two
words when one will do.
—Thomas Jefferson

───────────────────────────────────

HOW TO MAKE EVERY WORD COUNT

Speeches are meant to be heard, not read. That means you have
to keep your language simple and easily understood. Write for
the ear, not the eye.

Remember: Your audience will have only one shot to get
your message. They can't go back and reread a section that's
fuzzy, as they can with a book or a newspaper article. Get rid of
any fuzzy parts *before* you give the speech.

Never be content with your first draft. *Never.* After you've
written it, read it aloud.

Let some time elapse between your rewrites. Let the
whole thing sit overnight or over a couple of nights, if possible. Then go at it with a red pen. Cut ruthlessly. Simplify your
language.

This chapter will show you—in step-by-step detail—how
to simplify the language in your speech. It will help you:

- choose the right word

- simplify your phrases
- sharpen your sentences

Use Simple, Direct Words

Use the following list to make your own substitutions:

Instead of	*Try using*
abbreviate	shorten
accommodate	serve
advise	tell
aggregate	total, whole
anticipate	expect
approximately	about
ascertain	find out, figure out
burgeoning	growing
cessation	end
cognizant	aware
commencement	start, beginning
compel	make
component	part
conjecture	guess
currently	now
deceased	dead
demonstrate	show
desire	want
determine	find out
diminutive	little
discourse	talk
disseminate	spread
duplicate	copy
eliminate	cut out
elucidate	clarify
encounter	meet

endeavor	try
engage	hire
eradicate	wipe out
execute	do
expedite	speed
expire	die
facilitate	make easy
feasible	possible
forward	send
generate	make, cause
heretofore	until now
illustrate	show
indicate	say
initial	first
inquire	ask
locate	find
maintenance	upkeep
marginal	small
numerous	many
observe	see, watch
obtain	get
operate	work, use
originated	began
peruse	read
precipitate	cause
presently	soon
procure	get, take
recapitulate	sum up
recess	break
remunerate	pay
render	give, send
represents	is
require	need
reside	live
residence	home
retain	keep

review	check
saturate	soak
solicit	ask
stated	said
stringent	strict
submit	send
subsequent	next
substantial	large
sufficient	enough
supply	send
terminate	end
utilize	use
vacate	leave
vehicle	truck, car, van, bus
verification	proof

A final point: The Gettysburg Address is one of the world's most memorable speeches. Lincoln wrote 76 percent of it with words of *five letters or less*. Consider that an inspiration for you to do the same.

Avoid Jargon

> Infrastructure is the longest word any of us in politics have learned to say, so we say it a lot.
> —Carol Bellamy, former New York City Council president

Jargon doesn't work in a speech. It smacks of "bureaucratese" and audiences tend to block it out. It may even alienate some listeners. Get rid of it.

Jargon	*Plain English*
a guesstimate	a rough estimate
conceptualize	imagine
finalize	finish, complete

impact (verb)	affect
implement	carry out
infrastructure	foundation, framework
interface (verb)	talk with
meaningful	real
operational	okay, working
optimum	best
output	results
parameters	limits
utilization	use
viable	workable

Avoid Euphemisms

Euphemisms "bloat" a speech. Replace them with plain English.

Euphemism	*Plain English*
classification device	test
disadvantaged	poor
interrelated collectivity	group
inventory shrinkage	theft
motivational deprivation	laziness
negative patient care outcome	death
nomenclature	name
passed away	died
terminated	fired
unlawful or arbitrary deprivation of life	murder
unscheduled intensified repairs	emergency repairs

Avoid Vague Modifiers

Words such as "very," "slightly," and "extremely" are too vague to be useful. Use words or phrases that say *precisely* what you mean.

Vague	*Specific*
The personnel department is rather understaffed, but the situation will be corrected in the very near future.	The personnel department now has three vacancies. We will fill these jobs within the next month.

Don't Speak in Abbreviations

You may know what HEW, SEC, and FCC stand for, but don't assume that everyone else does.

You have to explain every abbreviation you use—not *every* time you use it, but at least the *first* time.

The same goes with acronyms, such as NOW for the National Organization for Women and PAC for political action committee. Unlike those abbreviations that are pronounced letter by letter (HEW, SEC, FCC, for example), acronyms are pronounced like words. You can use them in a speech, but be sure to identify them the first time.

This is a particular problem in the military, where initials and acronyms are regularly sprinkled throughout written communications—and often creep into oral presentations, as well. While other military folks might understand your abbreviations, the public at large finds them peculiar—even off-putting.

Root them out of your public presentations. You'll reach a lot more minds, persuade a lot more people, and make a lot more friends. Isn't that why you're speaking in the first place?

Don't Speak in Unfamiliar Languages

If you're an English-speaking native addressing an English-speaking audience, why would you want to throw in foreign phrases? To show the audience how educated you are? To impress them with your sophistication? To display a bit of class?

Forget it.

Not everyone in your audience will know the meaning of *pro bono publico*, *Wanderjahr*, or *chateaux en Espagne*. For that matter, you may not even know how to pronounce them properly, and that will make you appear foolish to the more knowledgeable members of your audience.

If you want to use a foreign proverb to illustrate a point, translate it into English. For example, "The French have a wonderful saying, 'The more things change, the more they stay the same.' This sentiment certainly describes our organization. We've served this community for fifty years. We've changed our structure along the way, but we haven't changed our goals."

On the other hand, *if you were born or reared in a foreign country*, you may use your native language to great effect.

Find an appropriate proverb from your native country . . . work it into your speech . . . offer it to the audience in your native tongue . . . pause . . . then give the English translation.

This well-timed delivery can greatly increase audience interest and help build emotional appeal.

When Jeffrey Steiner, chairman and CEO of the Fairchild Corporation, spoke on the five hundredth anniversary of the arrival of Jews in Turkey, he included a Yiddish proverb:

> When Sephardic Jews were expelled from Spain, they found a safe haven in Turkey. And, for half a millennium, Turkey has continued to extend a special benevolence to Jewish people fleeing persecution.
>
> I know. I was one of those people. During World War II, my family sought refuge in Turkey. We were able to escape the Nazis, and flee Vienna, and find safety in Istanbul. . . .

The history of the Jewish community in Turkey is remarkable. There is a Yiddish proverb that fits the spirit of our shared history, "Mountains cannot meet, but men can."

You see, for half a millennium, the republic of Turkey has proven that men and women of good will *can* meet . . . that tolerance and respect *can* cross the "mountains" of geographic borders . . . that people of different faiths *can* live together in harmony.

Avoid Sexist Language

There are several ways to avoid sexist implications in your speech.

Find substitutes for compound nouns that contain man or woman

This list should help:

businessmen	business people
cleaning woman	office cleaner
Congressmen	members of Congress
firemen	firefighters
foreman	supervisor
housewife	homemaker
insurance salesman	insurance agent
mailmen	mail carriers
man-hours	worker-hours
mankind	human beings
manpower	labor force
man's achievements	human achievements
policeman	police officer
political man	political behavior
repairman	repairperson/service rep
salesmen	sales reps, sales clerks, sales force
spokesman	spokesperson
statesman	leader
stewardess	flight attendant

Shift to the plural

Before	After
When a *manager* goes on a business trip, *he* should save all of *his* receipts.	When *managers* go on business trips, *they* should save all of *their* receipts.
A utility tax hits the *consumer* where *he* is already overburdened.	A utility tax hits *consumers* where *they* are already overburdened.

Restructure the sentence

Before	After
The company will select someone from the Treasury Department *to be chairman* of the Travel and Entertainment Committee.	The company will select someone from the Treasury Department *to head* the Travel and Entertainment Committee.

Alternate male and female examples

Before	After
Interviewers are too quick to say, *"He* doesn't have enough technical knowledge," or *"He's* just not the right *man* for us."	Interviewers are too quick to say, *"He* doesn't have enough technical knowledge," or *"She's* just not the right *person* for us."

Be sure that you don't always mention the male first. Switch the order: husbands and wives, hers or his, him or her, women and men.

Avoid male/female stereotypes

Doctors, nurses, and even astronauts come in both sexes. Do *not* refer to someone as a "female doctor" or a "male nurse." It's gratuitous.

SIMPLIFY YOUR PHRASES

> Everything should be made as simple as possible, but not simpler.
> —Albert Einstein

A phrase with too many words becomes meaningless. Look at your draft, and get rid of pompous, wordy, and overwritten constructions. Use the following list as a guideline:

Instead of	*Try using*
a large number of	many
a sufficient number of	enough
a total of 42	42
advance planning	planning
are in agreement with	agree with
as indicated in the following chart	the following chart shows
as you know	*Delete* (If they already know, why tell them?)
at that point in time	then
at the present time	now
at the time of presenting this speech	today
basically unaware of	did not know
be that as it may	but
blame it on	blame
both alike	alike
brief in duration	short
bring the matter to the attention of	tell
caused damage to	damaged
check into the facts	check the facts
consensus of opinion	consensus
continue on	continue
curiously enough	curiously

demonstrate the ability to	can
despite the fact that	although
due to the fact that	because
end product	product
equally as	equally
estimated at about	estimated at
exert a leadership role	lead
firm commitment	commitment
for free	free
for the purpose of	for
frame of reference	viewpoint, perspective
give encouragement to	encourage
have a discussion	discuss
hold a meeting	meet
hold in abeyance	suspend
in close proximity	near
in connection with	on, of
individuals who will participate	participants
in many cases	often
in order to	to
in some cases	sometimes
in the area of	approximately
in the course of	during
in the event of	if
in the majority of instances	most often, usually
in the vicinity of	near
in view of	because
is equipped with	has
is in an operational state	operates, works
is noted to have	has
is of the opinion that	thinks
it has been shown that	*Delete*
it is recognized that	*Delete*
it is recommended by me that	I recommend
it may be mentioned that	*Delete*

join together	join (unless in a marriage ceremony, where "join together" is acceptable)
made a complete reversal	reversed
make a decision	decide
my personal opinion	my opinion
needless to say	*Delete* (If you don't *need* to say it, why *would* you say it?)
never before in the past	never
new innovations	innovations
newly created	new
obtain an estimate of	estimate
off of	off
of sufficient magnitude	big enough
on a national basis	nationally
on the basis of	from
on the occasion of	when
optimum utilization	best use
over with	over
past experience	experience
personal friend	friend
predicated on	based on
prior to	before
provide assistance to	help
start off	start
study in depth	study
subsequent to	after
take action	act
the major portion	most
the reason why is that	because
until such time as	until
very unique	unique
was in communication with	talked with
with reference to	about
with regard to	about
with the exception of	except

with the result that	so that
would invoke an expenditure of	
approximately	would cost about

AVOID THE FLUFF PITFALL

If your speech is filled with statements such as, "This has been a most challenging year," or, "We all face a golden opportunity," or, "We will meet our challenges with optimism and view the future with confidence," it is probably high on fluff and low on content. Unfortunately, too many business speeches fall into this category.

To get rid of fluff, try this experiment. Listen to ten ordinary business speeches and count the number of times words such as "challenge" and "opportunity" are used. Pay careful attention to the opening and closing sections of the speeches, because that's where amateur writers tend to throw in the most fluff.

Then, listen to ten speeches that you can assume to be "ghostwritten"—speeches, for example, that are given by a top corporate president. These speeches will have fewer "challenges" and "opportunities" in their texts. Why? Because professional speechwriters try to avoid such fluff. They know that audiences block it out.

Follow the professionals. Review your speech and get rid of any glib expressions. If you want your message to stand out, put content—not fluff—into your speech.

SHARPEN YOUR SENTENCES

> When "whom" is correct, use some other formulation.
> —William Safire

There are several important things to know about sentences.

Short sentences are stronger than long sentences

Try this experiment: Take a sample page from your draft and count the number of words in each sentence. Write the numbers down and average them.

If you average twenty or more words per sentence, you'd better start cutting. Why? Because an audience can't follow what you're saying if you put too many words in a sentence. Your message just gets lost.

If you don't believe me, read your longest sentence aloud, then read your shortest sentence aloud. See which one is more powerful—and more memorable.

Variety is the spice of life

If all your sentences are long, no one will be able to follow you. But if all your sentences are short, your speech may become boring. People get tired of hearing the same rhythm. If you use a rather long sentence, precede or follow it with a short, punchy one. The contrast will catch your audience's attention.

FDR was a master of this technique, and his speeches show a great sense of rhythm and timing. Consider the following example. He uses a powerful, two-word sentence followed by a rhythmic, eighteen-word sentence:

> Hostilities exist. There is no mincing the fact that our people, our territory, and our interests are in grave danger.

Ronald Reagan also knew how to vary the rhythm of his speech:

> Everyone is against protectionism in the abstract. That is easy. It is another matter to make the hard, courageous choices when it is your industry or your business that appears to be hurt by foreign competition. I know. We in the United States deal with the problem of protectionism every day of the year.

Count the words he used: seven in the first sentence, then three, then twenty-six, then two, then sixteen. Average length? About eleven words per sentence.

Use the active, not the passive, voice

It's time for a grammar lesson. I'll keep it brief.

These sentences are in the *active voice* because they show that the subject acts, or does something:

- The Customer Inquiry Department *answers* almost four hundred phone calls every day.

- Our new maintenance program *saved* the company $5,000 in the first six months.

- The committee *records* all suggestions in a logbook.

- Government *must place* some constraints on these contracts to prevent price excesses.

A sentence is in the *passive voice* when the subject is acted upon:

- Almost four hundred phone calls *are answered* by the Customer Inquiry Department every day.

- Five thousand dollars *was saved* by the company in the first six months of our new maintenance program.

- All suggestions *are recorded* by the committee in a logbook.

- Some constraints *must be placed* on these contracts by government to prevent price excesses.

Read the above sentences aloud, and notice that the active voice:

1. sounds more vigorous

2. is more personal

3. uses fewer words

4. is easier to follow

5. is easier to remember

Get rid of passive constructions in your speech. They sound stilted, flat, and contrived.

Beware of adjectives

> Nouns and verbs are almost pure metal; adjectives are cheaper ore.
> —Marie Gilchrist

Try this test. Pick any two-to-three-page segment of your speech manuscript and underline the adjectives. Now, delete them—read the section out loud—and see if your speechwriting sounds crisper and stronger. If you really need those adjectives, fine, put them back in. If not? Just leave them out.

Cut "I think," "I believe," "I know," "It seems to me that," "In my opinion"

These expressions weaken sentences. Cut them, and you will make your sentences stronger.

Before	*After*
We think prices are already too high and we know people are hurting.	Prices are already too high and people are hurting.

Avoid "There are"

Sentences that begin with "There are . . ." are often weak. Try rewriting them.

Before	*After*
There are alternative ways that must be found by us to solve the problem.	We must find other ways to solve the problem.

Beware of tongue twisters

Read your speech aloud several times, and listen carefully for potential tongue twisters.

Try to round up a couple of junior high youngsters and have them listen to your speech. They are notorious for spotting potential tongue twisters, especially those that sound obscene. Better to have some junior high kids spot an embarrassing phrase than to have your audience laugh at it.

A QUICK SUMMATION

A bit of advice from George Orwell on how to make your writing simple:

1. Never use a long word where a short one will do.

2. If it is possible to cut out a word, always cut it out.

3. Never use the passive where you can use the active.

4. Never use a foreign phrase, a scientific word, or a jargon word if you can think of an everyday English equivalent.

5. Break any of these rules sooner than say anything barbarous.

THE ULTIMATE TEST

David Belasco, the great American theatrical producer, once said, "If you can't write your idea on the back of my calling card, you don't have a clear idea."

So, get out your business card, and see if you can put your main idea on the card. If it fits, wonderful. If not, maybe your idea is too flabby. Whittle. Cut.

SEVEN

Style

❋ ————————————————————————————————————

Poetry has everything to do with speeches—cadence,
rhythm, imagery, sweep, a knowledge that words are magic,
that words like children have the power to make dance the
dullest beanbag of a heart.

—Peggy Noonan

Business executives, military leaders, politicians, and civic
leaders give thousands of speeches every day. Most of these
speeches are forgotten as soon as the audience leaves the
room—if not sooner.

But, some speeches *do* linger in the minds and hearts of
audiences. What makes these speeches special? Style.

Speeches with style have a certain "ring" that makes them
easy to remember. They have a psychological appeal that
makes them seem *important* to remember. And they create an
impact that makes them irresistibly *quotable*.

Here are some techniques that professional speechwriters use.

HOW TO USE TRIPARTITE DIVISION

Tripartite division is a device that breaks things into three
parts. Three has always been a powerful number. Consider:

- the Holy Trinity

- the three wise men and their three gifts
- in children's literature: *Goldilocks and the Three Bears, The Three Little Pigs*, and *The Three Little Kittens*
- in baseball: Three strikes and you're out!
- from the battlefield: Ready! Aim! Fire!

For some mysterious reason, the human mind is strongly attracted to things that come in "three's." Throughout history, speakers have known that tripartite division is a powerful mnemonic device.

- *Julius Caesar,* "Veni, vidi, vici." ("I came, I saw, I conquered.")
- *Abraham Lincoln,* "We cannot dedicate, we cannot consecrate, we cannot hallow this ground."
- *Douglas MacArthur's farewell address at West Point,* "Duty, honor, country. Those three hallowed words reverently dictate what you ought to be, what you can be, what you will be."
- *President Reagan (in Normandy, on the anniversary of D-Day),* "The Soviet troops that came to the center of this continent did not leave when peace came. They are still there—uninvited, unwanted, unyielding, almost forty years after the war."

Admittedly these are some of the biggest names of history, but we ordinary people can make tripartite division work to our advantage, too.

- *A civic leader,* "The promise is there, the logic is overwhelming, the need is great."
- *The recipient of an award for community service,* "My volunteer work has been my life, my inspiration, my joy."

- *A bank manager,* "We do not wield the power we once did—power over our employees, our customers, our communities."

Triads are an easy way to add style to a presentation. When Pennsylvania governor Tom Ridge unveiled newly minted commemorative quarters in a ceremony at the U.S. Mint in Philadelphia, these triads helped make his speech as special as the occasion itself:

> Pennsylvania quarters aren't just quarters—they're tiny, silver reminders of Pennsylvania's past, Pennsylvania's pride, and Pennsylvania's promise. They tell our story, symbolize our heritage, and add to our legacy—all for 25 cents.

As president of the American Red Cross, Elizabeth Dole spoke at the Dartmouth College commencement in Hanover, New Hampshire—using this simple triad to create a pleasing style: "It is your moral compass that counts far more than any bank balance, any resume, and yes, any diploma."

HOW TO USE PARALLELISM

Use a parallel structure to create balance—the emotional appeal of harmony.

- *John Fitzgerald Kennedy,* "If a free society cannot help the many who are poor, it cannot save the few who are rich."

- *Richard Nixon,* "Where peace is unknown, make it welcome; where peace is fragile, make it strong; where peace is temporary, make it permanent."

HOW TO USE IMAGERY

Be specific, be vivid, be colorful—and you will make your point. Even better, your audience will *remember* your point.

- *Winston Churchill,* "An iron curtain has descended across the continent."

- *Franklin Delano Roosevelt,* "When you see a rattlesnake poised to strike, you do not wait until he has struck before you crush him."

- *President George Bush,* "The American symbol is an eagle, not an ostrich—and now is not the time to go burying our heads in the sand."

HOW TO USE INVERSION OF ELEMENTS

If you switch the elements in paired statements, you can produce some memorable lines.

- *John Fitzgerald Kennedy,* "Ask not what your country can do for you. Ask what you can do for your country."

- *A store owner,* "We would rather be a big fish in a small pond than a small fish in a big pond."

HOW TO USE REPETITION

Audiences do not always pay attention. Their minds wander. They think about the work that's piled up on their desks. They think about the bills that are piled up at home. They often miss whole sections of a speech.

If you have an important word or phrase or sentence, be sure to repeat it—again, and again. Jesse Jackson knew how to use this technique in his campaign speeches for the presidential nomination: "We must give peace a chance. We must give peace a chance. We must, we must!"

When H. Norman Schwarzkopf, hero of Operation Desert Storm, returned to the United States to deliver an address before the Joint Session of Congress, he used repetition to drive home a point with enormous power and pride:

> We were all volunteers and we were regulars. We were Reservists and we were National Guardsmen, serving side by side as we have in every war, because that's what the U.S. military is.
>
> And, we were men and women, each of us bearing our fair share of the load and none of us quitting because the conditions were too rough or the job was too tough, because that's what your military is.
>
> We were Protestants and Catholics and Jews and Moslems and Buddhists and many other religions fighting for a common and just cause, because that's what your military is.
>
> We were black and white and yellow and brown and red, and we noticed when our blood was shed in the desert it didn't separate by race but it flowed together, because that's what your military is. . . .

Read Winston Churchill aloud to sense the full power of repetition:

> We shall fight in France, we shall fight on the seas and oceans, we shall fight with growing confidence and strength in the air, we shall defend our island, whatever the cost may be, we shall fight on the beaches, we shall fight in the fields and in the streets, we shall fight in the hills; we shall never surrender.

HOW TO USE RHETORICAL QUESTIONS

Ask rhetorical questions to *involve* your audience. Pause a moment or so after each question. This will allow listeners some time to answer the question in their own minds—and it will help reinforce your message.

- *Grammy-winning singer k.d. lang* (on behalf of animal rights), "We all love animals, but why do we call some of them pets and some of them dinner?"

- *Comedian Jay Leno,* "Iraq attacks Kuwait, there's an upheaval in Liberia, there's an attempted coup in the Philippines. . . . You ever get the feeling that the Goodwill Games just didn't work out this year?"

- Bill Cosby, challenging the media's effect on children, "The networks say they don't influence anybody. If that's true, why do they have commercials? Why am I sitting there with Jell-O pudding?"

HOW TO USE CONTRAST

Sharpen your point with contrasting words. Opposites pack a verbal punch—boosting audience comprehension, and enhancing your delivery.

At a commemoration honoring Martin Luther King Jr., President George W. Bush said, "Some figures in history, renowned in their day, grow smaller with the passing of time. The man from Atlanta, Georgia, only grows larger with the years."

HOW TO USE RHYTHM

Cadence drives your message into the minds of the listeners. When President Bush addressed the Congress on the end of the Gulf War, he closed with these stirring words:

> . . . this victory belongs to them—to the privates and the pilots, to the sergeants and the supply officers, to the men and women in the machines, and the men and women who made them work. It belongs to the regulars, to the reserves, to the guard. This victory belongs to the finest fighting force this nation has ever known.

We went halfway around the world to do what is moral and just and right. We fought hard, and—with others—we won the war.

We're coming home now—proud. Confident—heads high. There is much that we must do at home and abroad. And we will do it. We are Americans.

HOW TO USE VIVID WORDS

Franklin Delano Roosevelt is forever identified with this memorable line about Pearl Harbor, "This was a day that will live in infamy." Few people know, however, that the original draft of his speech read, "This is a day that will live in world history." FDR used the power of the pen (literally).

If you're hoping to generate media coverage for your speeches, vivid words can make all the difference. When I teach master-level seminars in speechwriting, I encourage the participants to make their speeches as "quotable" as possible—and word play does the trick.

Word play doesn't have to be complex. In fact, the best word play is disarmingly simple. One quick change, one new syllable, and—voilà! You have a quotable line.

Complaining about President Clinton to a meeting of the Christian Coalition, New Hampshire senator Bob Smith said, "We have a character in the White House. We need character in the White House."

When the FBI received criticism for taking too long to investigate the crash of TWA Flight 800, Assistant FBI Director James Kallstrom defended the lengthy probe: "We had to look at every dark crack and crevice in this investigation. We are the Federal Bureau of Total Investigation . . . not the Federal Bureau of the Obvious."

The president of the Public Relations Society of America, Mary Lynn Cusick APR, changed one-half of a compound word to summarize the tasks facing public relations professionals: "We need to be evaluating outcomes, not output."

EIGHT

Humor: What Works, What Doesn't, and Why

✳ ────────────────────────────────

Once you get people laughing, they're listening and you can
tell them almost anything.
—Herbert Gardner

────────────────────────────────────

Some people think they absolutely must use a joke to begin a
speech. I hope you are not one of these people.

Jokes can be risky. There's nothing worse than a joke that
falls flat—unless it's a joke that falls flat at the beginning of a
speech. Beware.

Ask yourself five questions before you plan to use a joke
anywhere in your speech:

- "Will this joke tie into the subject and mood of my
  speech?"

- "Will my audience feel comfortable with this joke?"

- "Is the joke short and uncomplicated?"

- "Is the joke fresh?"

- "Can I deliver this joke really well—with confidence
  and ease and perfect timing?"

If you can't answer "yes" to all of these questions, scrap the
joke.

USE A LIGHT TOUCH

Professional comedians like jokes that produce loud laughs. But you are a speaker, not a professional comedian.

Don't focus on jokes that beg for loud laughs because this usually backfires. Instead, try to develop a "light touch" of humor. You can do this through:

- personal anecdotes
- one-liners that blend into the speech
- humorous quotations
- quips that seem off-the-cuff (but are actually planned)
- clever statistics
- word play
- gestures
- voice intonations
- raising an eyebrow
- smiling

Using a light touch of humor will help the audience to see you as a decent, humane, and friendly person. It will help put the audience in a receptive mood for the message of your speech.

WHAT WORKS

What kind of humor works best in a speech? The kind that is friendly, personal, and natural. Humor in a speech doesn't need to produce guffaws. A few smiles and some chuckles are just fine for your purpose.

Where can you find this humor? Many speakers buy

books of jokes and adapt the material to suit their own needs. These sources can be helpful, but *only* if you use them judiciously. *Don't* use the material verbatim. Always adapt the humor to your own needs and your own style.

Learn to create *your own* light touches of humor. Original material will work better than material that is lifted straight from books.

Why? Three big reasons:

1. If you create your own humorous touches, you can be sure this material will be fresh to your audience.

2. If the humor comes from your own experience, you will deliver it more naturally and more effectively.

3. If you share something personal with the audience, they will feel more friendly toward you.

Your safest bet for good humor in a speech is to poke gentle fun at yourself. Try making light of:

- *Your fame.* A little boy once asked John F. Kennedy how he became a war hero. "It was absolutely involuntary," Kennedy replied. "They sank my boat."

- *Your image.* When President George W. Bush laid plans to sign landmark education reforms, he quipped that he would share the stage with his long-time political opposite, Sen. Edward Kennedy: "A lot of my friends in Midland, Texas, are going to be amazed when I stand up and say nice things about Ted Kennedy."

- *Popular opinion.* When rumors swirled in the early 1980s that Lee Iacocca might run for president of the United States, he addressed the issue in his own, inimitable style: "All this talk about me running for president is becoming a problem. It distracts from the Chrysler story—and it gets my campaign staff upset."

- *Your speaking persona.* Alan Greenspan, chairman of
  the Federal Reserve Board, made this quip when he
  spoke at the Economic Club in New York: "I guess I
  should warn you: If I turn out to be particularly clear,
  you've probably misunderstood what I've said."

A Caution

Poking fun at yourself is the safest kind of humor, but never
belittle your professional competence in your area of expertise.
Otherwise, the audience will wonder why they should bother
listening to you.

Never say anything about yourself that you might regret
later. A speech is over in fifteen or twenty minutes, but a reputation lasts a lifetime. Don't sacrifice a reputation for a
cheap laugh.

WHAT ARE YOUR CHANCES
OF GETTING A LAUGH?

You'll find it's easier to get a laugh as the day goes on. Why?
Because it's usually easier to get *anything* as the day goes on.

Think about it:

Early in the morning, people are still groggy. Their minds
often aren't working well. If they think about anything at all,
they think about the pile of work that lies ahead of them. They
just want to have a cup of coffee and get moving with their
schedule. They're not in a very playful mood—and it's hard to
be funny when the audience doesn't want to play along.

So, if you're the guest speaker at a breakfast fund-raiser,
for example, keep everything short and simple. Even if the
audience is really interested in your cause, they will be anxious
to get out of the meeting and get on with the day's work. No

complicated jokes, please. A quick one-liner is probably all these people can handle.

By lunchtime, things ease up a bit. At least some of the day's work is done, and people can sit back and relax a little. Still, they have to get back to the office, and they will be looking at their watches as two o'clock approaches.

By dinnertime, things are as loose as they'll ever be. Work is over. People want to put their troubles behind them for a while. They're in the mood to unwind. Indulge them. Give them the chuckles they *want*.

By late evening, however, things may be *too* loose for humor to work. In fact, things may be too loose for *anything* to work—including the speaker! By ten or eleven o'clock, most audiences are either too inattentive, too inebriated, or too tired to be receptive to any message.

At this late hour, you must put aside your ego and put aside your prepared speech—no matter how witty or wise that speech might be.

Just give a three-or-four-sentence capsule summary, flash a broad smile, and get out of there. The audience will love you for it.

WHAT ABOUT DELIVERY?

A good delivery will greatly increase your chances of getting a good laugh.

You must be in complete control of the joke or anecdote. You must understand every word, every pause, every nuance. You must—above all—have a good sense of timing.

Want to see how important good delivery is? Practice this fifth-century line from Saint Augustine: "Give me chastity and continence, but not just now." The pause after "continence" makes the whole line.

Don't set yourself up for failure by announcing, "Here's a really funny story." Let the audience decide for themselves if it's really funny or not.

Be prepared in case the audience thinks it *isn't* funny. The only thing worse than the silence that follows a failed joke is the sound of the speaker laughing while the audience sits in embarrassed silence. Don't laugh at your own jokes. As Archie Bunker used to say to Edith, "Stifle yourself."

Special-Occasion Speeches

✳

Act well your part: there all the honor lies.
—Alexander Pope

Not all speeches deal with big issues. Many speeches are simply ceremonial. They honor a person's retirement, or present an award, or dedicate a new building.

These speeches are different from the standard public speech. They're usually much shorter, and they often take a personal approach.

This chapter will give some guidelines on:

- the invocation

- the commencement speech

- the award or tribute speech

It will also help you with some specialized speaking skills:

- How to introduce a speaker.

- How to give an impromptu speech.

- How to organize a panel presentation.

- How to present as a team.

- How to handle a question-and-answer session.

THE INVOCATION

The fewer words, the better prayer.
—Martin Luther

The scene: You're sitting on a dais at a banquet. The evening's event? To honor a local business executive with a humanitarian award.

Just before the banquet begins, the master of ceremonies learns that the clergyman who was supposed to offer the invocation can't attend. They need someone to fill in, and they turn to you. "Would you be kind enough to offer grace?"

Well, *would* you? Even more to the point, *could* you?

Could you come up with an invocation that's appropriate for a mixed business gathering—a gathering that might include Christians, Jews, Muslims, and others?

Avoid prayers that represent a specific religious preference.

A decidedly Christian prayer, for example, might exclude some parts of the audience. What's worse, it might even *offend* some parts of the audience. I am reminded of an unfortunate invocation that ended with, "We pray for this in Jesus' name." Well, the Jewish man sitting next to me certainly wasn't praying in Jesus' name—and he resented the arrogance of the person who gave that prayer.

Don't give an invocation that might alienate some people in your audience. Instead, come up with something that shows respect for all people—something that honors human dignity.

In a business setting, it's appropriate to:

- give thanks for all blessings

- pray for peace

- ask for wisdom and courage and strength to deal with your problems

Above all, keep it short—under a minute, if you can. A word of caution about humorous invocations: *don't*. This is not the time to use a light touch. Avoid *anything* such as "Good food, good meat, good God, let's eat." (Yes, I'm told someone actually used that invocation at a civic organization.)

THE COMMENCEMENT SPEECH

Proclaim not all thou knowest.
—Benjamin Franklin.

Everyone is in a good mood at a commencement. Students are glad to be finished with exams. Parents are glad to be finished with tuition bills. And instructors are glad to be finished with another academic year.

Don't let long-winded or pompous remarks put them in a bad mood.

Remember: Caps and gowns can be hot. Folding chairs can be uncomfortable. Crowded gymnasiums can be unbearably stuffy. Follow Franklin Delano Roosevelt's advice: "Be brief; be sincere; be seated."

In the process, of course, try to say something inspirational, thoughtful, encouraging, uplifting, or memorable. The Academy Award–winning actress Meryl Streep knew this when she returned to speak at her alma mater, Vassar College. She encouraged the graduates to strive for excellence, even though life might be difficult at times. "If you can live with the devil," Streep said, "then Vassar has not sunk its teeth into you." This proved to be a great line for a commencement speech—easy for the audience to remember, and irresistible for the press to quote.

It's safest to speak for between ten and fifteen minutes. If you go on longer, the audience may get dangerously restless. After all, a graduating class doesn't have to worry anymore about reprisals from the school principal or the college president. They're free to yawn or talk or even boo. Don't make any remarks about the brevity (or verbosity) of your speech. I once heard a commencement speaker promise to be brief. He was, much to his embarrassment, applauded by a few rambunctious students.

Remember that June weather is notoriously fickle. If the commencement is outdoors, be alert to the storm clouds and be prepared to shorten your address if the rains come.

Also, make sure your hat's on tight. More than one commencement speaker has been embarrassed by a hat flying off into the wind.

PRESENTING AN AWARD

'Tis an old maxim in the schools,
That flattery's the food of fools;
Yet now and then your men of wit
Will condescend to take a bit.
—Jonathan Swift

A person who retires after forty years of service, an employee who contributes a money-saving idea to the company, and a telephone installer who saves a customer's life, all of these people deserve some special recognition, and you may be asked to give a speech in honor of one of them.

These five guidelines should help:

1. *Be generous with the praise.* If one of your employees risked his life to save a customer's life and he's now receiving a special award, you must come up with praise to match the occasion. Be generous.

2. *Be specific.* Whatever you say should be so specific that it couldn't possibly be said about anyone else. Never, *never* give an award speech that sounds "canned."
   For example, if the person is retiring after forty

years with the company, mention two or three specific projects he was involved in. Tell how his involvement made a difference.

3. *Be personal.* Make your tribute reveal a flesh-and-blood person. Show the honoree's personality and vulnerability.

    One good way to personalize your presentation: Ask the honoree's friends and family for some special recollections. Include a few of these "real-life" stories when you make your presentation.

4. *Be sincere.* Suppose you must give an award to a person you've never met. Don't pretend to be a close friend or associate. Simply get some information about the person from a supervisor and share this information in a sincere, straightforward way.

    For example, "Karen's supervisor has told me how Karen saved a baby's life. I'm glad to meet Karen and to present her with this award for distinguished service. I'm proud to have her as one of our employees."

5. *Be inspirational.* The Reverend Peter Gomes said this in a memorial tribute to Martin Luther King Jr. at Harvard University: "We remember Martin Luther King Jr. not because of his success, but because of our failures; not because of the work he has done, but because of the work we must do."

INTRODUCING A SPEAKER

Your assignment is to introduce a speaker. That's simple. Just call the speaker and ask for a written introduction—not a resume or a vita, but a completely written introduction that you can deliver.

What a Good Introduction Should Include

A good introduction should be brief—certainly no more than three minutes, and preferably just a minute or two.
It will let the audience know:

- Why it is that *this speaker*
- from *this organization*
- is talking about *this topic*
- to *this audience*
- at *this time*.

A good introduction should present this information in a friendly, personal way. It should *not* sound like a resume. It should *not* sound like a repetition of the biographical data already printed on the program.

If the speaker provides you with a stuffy introduction, rewrite it to sound friendlier. For example, delete a boring list of professional organizations and fill in with an anecdote that shows what kind of person the speaker is.

If the introduction provided is too modest, add some material that shows the speaker's unique qualifications. Quote the speaker, if possible, or quote someone else's remarks showing the speaker's special attributes.

Introduction dos

- Be sure to pronounce the speaker's name correctly. (Verify the pronunciation in advance.)

- Repeat the speaker's name several times during the introduction so the audience can catch it.

- At the end of the introduction, face the audience (*not* the speaker) and announce the speaker's name, "We couldn't have found a more qualified hospital administrator than—Peggy Smith."

- Then turn to the speaker and smile.

- In formal situations, applaud until the speaker reaches your side, shake hands, and return to your place.

- In informal situations, sit down as soon as the speaker rises and starts toward the lectern.

- Pay close attention to the speaker's opening. It may contain a reference to you, and you should be prepared to smile or nod in response.

- Plan these movements carefully. Make sure the speaker knows the last line of your introduction so he or she can use it as a cue.

Introduction don'ts

- Don't upstage the speaker by making your introduction *too* funny. (Let the speaker be the star.)

- Don't try to present a capsule summary of the speaker's speech. (You might misinterpret the speaker's focus, and that would put the speaker at a serious disadvantage.)

- Don't steal the speaker's material. (If the speaker told you a good anecdote over lunch last week, don't use it. The speaker might have planned to use it in the speech.)

- Don't rely on memory. (Write out your introduction in full.)

- Don't ad-lib. (Many a "spontaneous" comment has turned into an inane one—especially after a few drinks.)

- Don't draw attention to any negative conditions. (For example, don't say, "We're glad that Josephine has recovered from her heart attack and that she can be with us today." Comments like this do *not* put an audience in a relaxed mood.)

- Don't try to con the audience by saying things such as, "This is the funniest speaker you'll ever hear." (Let the audience make up their own minds.)

- Don't put pressure on the speaker by saying, "Now we'll see whether or not he's an excellent speaker, which I expect he is." (I once heard a CEO make such an introduction, and the speaker looked terrified.)

Five Cliches That Never Work in an Introduction

These cliches do a disservice to you and to the poor speaker who must follow your introduction. Avoid:

1. "Ladies and gentlemen: here is a speaker who needs no introduction. . . ."

2. "Her reputation speaks for itself. . . ."

3. "Without further ado . . ."

4. "Ladies and gentlemen: heeeere's . . ."

5. "We are a lucky audience to get anyone willing to substitute at the last moment . . ."

I have heard all these introductions used by supposedly intelligent people. I wished I had not, and so did the rest of the audience.

A Tacky Introduction

How many times have you heard someone stand up on a banquet dais and say, "I'd like to introduce Mr. John Jones and his good wife, Nancy"?

What, exactly, is a "good" wife? If John Jones had a "bad" wife, would the host announce that, too?

Get rid of "the good wife" or "the better half." Such phrases are tacky and belittling. Just say, "I'd like to introduce John and Nancy Jones."

THE IMPROMPTU SPEECH

Mark Twain once said, "It takes three weeks to prepare a good ad-lib speech." Alas, he was right. If you're going to a meeting where someone *might* ask you to speak, gather your thoughts in advance.

Ask yourself, "What is likely to happen at this meeting? Who will be there? What will they probably say? Are there any controversial areas? Will people have questions for me? How should I respond?"

Make notes about the topics you think will come up. Practice some impromptus until you are comfortable and convincing. Be sure to practice *aloud*. Your thoughts can't count until they're spoken—and heard.

Perhaps the worst thing that can happen at a meeting is for someone to ask you for an answer, opinion, or analysis, and the request catches you totally off guard. You've never given the subject a thought. You don't have any facts or figures. You're in deep trouble, right?

Not necessarily. If you have poise, your audience will forgive you almost anything. Keep your head high, your back straight, your shoulders relaxed, your eyes alert, your voice strong, your pitch moderate.

Above all, don't apologize. Never say anything like, "Oh, I'm so sorry. I feel so embarrassed. I didn't know you'd ask me to speak. I don't have any information with me."

No one expects you to give a keynote address under these circumstances. Just make a comment. If you can't come up with an intelligent response, keep your poise, maintain direct eye contact, and say, in an even voice, "I don't know. I will look into that and get back to you with the information."

How to Organize an Impromptu Speech

- Decide what you want to talk about—*fast!*

- Commit yourself to that approach. Don't change subjects or reverse your opinion midstream.

- Feel free to pause for a few seconds to collect your thoughts. The audience will not think you're stupid; they'll admire you for being able to organize your ideas under difficult circumstances.

- Open with a generalization to stall for time, if necessary. "Deregulation is certainly an important issue right now" will buy you a few extra seconds to compose your response.

- Or, repeat the question to stall for extra time. "You're asking me about the changes that deregulation will bring to our industry." Repeating the question has an extra benefit: It makes sure the audience knows what you've been asked to speak about.

- Present just two or three points of evidence. Do not bore the audience with chronological details.

- Wrap up your impromptu speech with a firm conclusion—a punch line that people can focus on.

- Do not ramble. Once you've offered what sounds like a conclusion, just stop.

PANEL PRESENTATIONS

How to Moderate

- Seat the panelists three or four minutes in advance—just long enough to allow them to get their papers in order.

- Make sure they have glasses of water, with extra pitchers on the table. Also make sure they have stopwatches.

- Use large name cards to identify the panelists (by first and last names).

- Start the presentation on time.

- Introduce yourself right away. I once heard a moderator, an editor, ramble on for seventeen minutes before she gave her name. The members of the audience kept whispering to each other, "Who is she? Who is she?" I'm sure they were also wondering, "What's she doing up there?"

- Make sure the audience is comfortable. If people are standing at the back of the room, tell them there are seats available at the front, then pause and allow them to move forward. If you don't take care of these logistics at the beginning, you'll be bothered by rustling noises throughout the panel presentation.

- As you introduce the panelists, use their names two or three times. Unless you are introducing J.D. Salinger, do *not* use initials. Give everyone a first name.

- Tell the purpose of the panel presentation.

- Explain *how* the panel will work (number of minutes allowed for each panelist, time for rebuttals, questions and answers, etc.).

- Give the panelists a "thirty-second signal" so they can wrap up their presentations. One effective technique is to simply show the panelist a 3" × 5" card that reads "30 seconds."

- If panelists run overtime, interrupt them—nicely, of course—and give them fifteen seconds to finish.

- *Do not* let any panelist abuse your schedule. Say in a firm, even voice, "Thank you, Mrs. Smith, but your time is up."

- Close the presentation on schedule with a few words of thanks to the panelists and to the audience.

How to Be a Panelist

- Be prepared for the worst. Inexperienced moderators may not know the above guidelines. Try to make the best of the situation.

- If the moderator forgot name cards or didn't pronounce your name properly, start by saying, "Hello. I'm *(name)*."

- If the moderator didn't give you an adequate introduction, briefly give your credentials and explain why you're there.

- Give your presentation a good title. This accomplishes several things: First, it clarifies your specific role on the panel; second, it sets the tone of your message; and third, it presents a more professional speaking image.

    Anthony Santomero, president of the Federal Reserve Bank of Philadelphia, used this straightforward title when he spoke at the National Association for Business Economics: "What Monetary Policy Can and Cannot Do."

- If you are the last speaker and the time has run out, know how to give a shortened presentation.

- If another panelist refuses to stop speaking and the moderator can't control the situation, you may be forced to assert yourself. Take heart from Maxine Waters, the state legislator from Los Angeles. When Sen. Gary Hart was trying to woo delegates to the National Women's Political Caucus convention in San Antonio, he supposedly ignored five warnings that his time was up. Maxine Waters, one of the panelists, finally demanded, "What does your refusal to relinquish the podium say about your attitude toward women?" What, indeed?

Some Tips for Team Presentations

For many organizations, team presentations have become a way of life. Certainly, a well-orchestrated team presentation can pack a real wallop—but it also poses serious pitfalls. Know what you're dealing with.

Here are some suggestions:

Prior to the presentation:

1. *Make one person responsible.* This team leader will need to manage the entire project—from initial brainstorming sessions to final dress rehearsals.

2. *Set the date for your dress rehearsal.* Do this up front—and make it firm. What's the best time to rehearse? One full day prior to the actual presentation. You want enough time for speakers to make *minor* changes to their material or slides—but not enough time to fall into the temptation of making *major* changes! (This is one of the biggest problems I've seen as a speech coach. Speakers get to the rehearsal and frantically decide to rewrite their whole presentation—leaving no time for practice.)

3. *Hire a presentation coach early in the process.* Good speech coaches are booked well in advance. Don't wait until the last minute to hire yours.

4. *Keep everyone informed.* Keep everyone in the loop for meeting schedules, content themes, visual concepts, production deadlines, handout requirements, and rehearsal schedules.

5. *Clarify each person's function in writing.* It isn't enough for Bob to know what he's supposed to do. Everyone else has to know what Bob should do as well. "Who's doing the PowerPoint?" is a question you never want to hear. Prevent confusion by writing clear, direct "to do" lists—with no wiggle room.

6. *Capitalize on the unique strengths of your team.* Who has the most pleasing voice? Choose that person to welcome the audience. Who has the strongest storytelling skills? Tap that person to kick off your presentation with a riveting example. Who's the most persuasive person? Ask her to present controversial material. Who has the best technical skills? Have him handle any demonstrations. Who knows the audience best? Let him moderate the questions and answers.

7. *Work around weaknesses.* If Sue typically spends too much time explaining the charts, let someone else do that section of the presentation.

8. *Build continuity.* Make sure each speaker's message connects with the rest of the team. Use smooth transitions. Ruthlessly cut duplication. (Your team members should *reinforce* each other—not *repeat* each other. There's a difference.)

9. *Incorporate a series of deadlines.* Multiple deadlines keep everyone on track—and assure a better final product. Dress rehearsals are *not* the time to learn that Sam based his presentation on faulty research.

10. *Plan the dress rehearsal carefully.* Pay attention to timing. Multiple pass-offs can be time-consuming, and technology demonstrations often take longer than anticipated.

At the presentation:

1. *Get every presenter settled at the same time.* If three team members arrive on stage at 9:15, but the fourth team member doesn't arrive until almost 9:30, well, that sends a signal to the audience—a bad signal.

2. *Give each member a good introduction.* You'll find detailed advice about "introductions" in my earlier book, *Can You Say a Few Words?* (St. Martin's Press, 1991).

3. *Listen to each other's presentations.* Active listening means: good eye contact, attentive body language, appropriate smiles, and occasional nods of agreement.

4. *Control the question-and-answer session carefully.* It's embarrassing when one presenter gets all the questions, while the rest of the team just sits there like well-dressed mannequins. Encourage participation. You want your Q&A to have a "team spirit," and to flow as smoothly as the presentation itself.

QUESTION-AND-ANSWER SESSIONS

> There aren't any embarrassing questions—just
> embarrassing answers.
> —Ambassador Carl T. Rowan Jr.

A question-and-answer session can make or break your speech. Plan to make the Q&A work *for* you, not *against* you.

You should prepare for a Q&A as carefully as you prepare for a speech. Always develop a list of possible questions. Be realistic. If you're giving a speech on a controversial topic, you can expect to receive some tough questions.

Consult with the people in your business who work close to the news—for example, the consumer advocate, the treasurer, the public relations staff. Have them review your list of possible questions. Ask them to add to it.

Don't be intimidated by the difficulty of these questions. Don't allow yourself to be placed in a defensive position. Instead, come up with answers that work to *your* advantage. Practice these answers—*aloud*. It doesn't do any good to plan an assertive response if you can't sound assertive when you give it.

Here are ten practical tips to help you with a question-and-answer session:

1. *Take questions from all parts of the audience.*

2. *Listen carefully to each question.*   Don't smile or frown excessively as you listen—save your response until it's time for you to answer. Don't nod your head enthusiastically to show you understand the question. The audience may think you automatically agree with the question.

3. *Pay attention to your posture and body language.* Avoid any fidgeting motions that might reveal anxiety. Never, for example, click a pen while you are being asked a question.

4. *Treat every questioner as an equal.*   Don't try to compliment someone by saying, "Good question." It implies the others were *not* good questions. Be especially careful not to "brush off" questions from your subordinates or to fawn over comments from your superiors.

5. *Repeat all positive questions.*   This makes sure the audience has heard the question. It also buys you a few seconds of time to prepare your response.

6. *Paraphrase the negative questions.*   This allows you to set the tone and to control the emphasis of your answer. *Don't* repeat any hostile language, e.g., "Why did we fire all the older workers who had been with the company for so many years?" If you repeat it, you might be quoted as actually saying it.

7. *Look first at the person who asked the question.* Then establish good eye contact with the whole audience as you give the answer.

8. *Respond simply and directly.* If your response is too long, the audience may think you're trying to stall for time to avoid further questions.

9. *Don't extend your answers.* The more you say, the more chance you have to hang yourself. Remember what Calvin Coolidge said, "I have never been hurt by anything I didn't say."

10. *Don't limit yourself by saying, "This will be our last question."* If that question turns out to be a difficult one and you handle it poorly, you will end in a needlessly weak position. Instead, try saying, "We have a few minutes left. Can I take another question?" If you feel confident with the answer you give, then let this be the last question and wrap up the session. If you aren't satisfied to end the session at this point, you still have the option of accepting another question.

How to Handle Special Problems in a Q&A Session

- *If no one asks you a question.* Don't just stand there in silence. Ask yourself a question. Try, "Last week, when I spoke to the Chamber of Commerce, several people asked me about our plans to build a new plant. Perhaps I should spend a few minutes on that."

- *If someone asks about something you already discussed in the speech.* Answer anyway. Perhaps you didn't make your message clear enough. Try another approach. If you used an anecdote to explain something during your speech, use statistics or quotations to clarify the point during your Q&A. If the audience didn't understand your first technique, maybe they'll understand your second or third.

• *If someone repeats a question that's already been asked.* Don't answer it again. "I believe we've already answered that" will usually work.

• *If someone tries to turn a question into a long-winded speech.* Stop him or her politely but firmly. Interrupt the person's rambling and ask him or her to come to the point and give the question—"in the interest of saving time." The rest of the audience will appreciate this indication that you value their time. Gestures can help. When you interrupt the questioner, raise your hand in front of you. This "stop sign" signal will reinforce your words.

• *If someone asks a totally irrelevant question (perhaps about your personal life).* Just say, "Well, that's not what we're here to discuss."—period—end of discussion.

• *If someone asks a disorganized question.* Respond to only one part and ignore the rest. Naturally, pick the part of the question that will help you to reinforce your message.

• *If you don't know the answer.* Say so. Offer to get the information and send it to the person.

• *If you run out of time.* Say you're sorry you couldn't get to answer every question. Offer to make yourself available to people who want to pursue the subject further—perhaps during a coffee break or during a cocktail hour.

How to Respond to Hostile Questions

You're the manager of consumer conservation at an electric utility, and you've just finished speaking to a community group about energy-saving ideas. Up pops a hand, and you hear this question: "How can you stand there and talk about conservation when thousands of old people in your service area are so poor that they can't even eat? What do you want them to do? Pay high rates and eat cat food?"

How do you get out of this one? Very carefully.

Hostile questions are *not* impossible to answer. They just require special skills. Learn the techniques and practice them. Do it now, before you need to use these skills. Don't wait until you're put on the spot. It's too late then.

Start by giving yourself three basic rights:

- the right to be treated fairly
- the right to stay in control—of yourself and the situation
- the right to get your message across correctly

Remember: You are the invited speaker. No one in the audience has the right to take your role or to obscure your message.

Concentrate on getting your message across. In preparation for any Q&A, choose two or three important points that you can express as one-liners. Memorize these lines. Use them as *focus statements* when the Q&A gets difficult.

Rephrase any hostile questions so you can get into a *focus statement*.

For example:

Q: "All of your fancy plans to put up these big apartment buildings will just tear up our streets and tear down our old homes. What do you want to do to our downtown area? Kill it?"

A: "You're asking about our redevelopment plans." (rephrased question) *"Well, let me say that we plan to build a healthy downtown—where people can live and where businesses can do business."* (focus statement)

Don't be afraid of hostile questions. As Edmund Burke put it, "He who opposes me, and does not destroy me, strengthens me."

It's also imperative that you never insult anyone. "Well, I'd never insult anyone in a question-and-answer session. That would be mean—and dangerous." Is this what you're thinking to yourself?

You're right. It *would* be mean and dangerous to insult anyone during a Q&A. But unthinking speakers do it all the time. Let me share a few bad examples so you can learn from their lessons.

Q: "Why is the company authorizing so much stock? That's way too much!"

A: "Do you know the difference between issued and authorized stock? Issued stock is . . ."

Q: "Are you saying I don't know what I'm talking about!"

Don't accidentally insult a questioner's intelligence. Listen respectfully to the question, then try, "For the benefit of the whole audience, let me explain the difference between *issued* and *authorized* stock."

Q: "Why didn't you do more testing on that drug before you sold it to the public?"

A: "If you'd been listening to my speech, you'd obviously know the answer to that question."

Don't embarrass questioners in public. They will never forget the humiliation, and they will hold it against you.

Warning: "Obviously" can be an emotionally charged word. It often seems like a put-down. After all, if something was so obvious, why did the questioner miss it? Is he or she stupid?

* * *

A heckler dominated the Q&A session at an important meeting. The speaker grew increasingly frustrated, and finally threatened the heckler with, "I'm going to ask you to sit down in a few minutes."

Of course, the heckler just loved this attention, so he continued to interrupt the Q&A with long-winded questions. Each time, the speaker raised his voice and said, "I'm going to ask you to sit down soon."

Don't make idle threats. The heckler will love the extra attention, and the audience will think you are ineffectual. If you can't carry out a threat, don't make it.

Q: "Why do you think your program is so much better than the one Fred Smith started, which we've been using for years?"

A: "Well, there were lots of problems with the old program. For example, . . ."

Don't criticize a predecessor's work. Even if Fred is no longer with the organization, he may have friends and relatives and loyal supporters who still are. They will resent you for knocking his work.

Instead, explain that you inherited a fine structure, but that new information, subsequent events, increased funding, larger staff, or advanced technology allowed you to build on that foundation. For a strong emotional appeal, point out how Fred himself would have probably welcomed the chance to expand his original program: "At Fred's retirement dinner, he said the future seemed to be coming faster and faster—and that he wished he could be around to see all the changes in our industry."

Never give the impression that you've disregarded someone else's work, or the audience will think you are reckless and arrogant.

Tips for Television Interviews .

> In the age of soundbites, the three-minute Gettysburg Address
> would have been two-and-a-half minutes too long. One of
> today's ambitious young correspondents would probably have
> summed it up this way: "The President himself admitted to this
> subdued Pennsylvania crowd what his men have been saying
> privately: That no one will long remember what he said here."
> —Richard M. Nixon

Television brings us a wide range of morning interview shows, evening news programs, the late-night news, special crisis reports, weekly news analyses, profiles of executives, coverage of community events, local business updates, hard-hitting exposés, consumer advisories, and insider stories.

Of course, to keep all this news coverage running, television needs *people who will appear as guests*. Question: Will *you* be sitting in one of those interview chairs someday?

There are two basic ways to appear on TV:

1. Perhaps you'll be invited to promote something you're proud of. Some common situations:

• An executive is eager to appear on TV so she can publicize a new sales effort.

• A civic leader needs visibility so he can create support for a worthwhile community project.

• A high-school principal welcomes the chance to talk about a unique educational experiment.

2. On the other hand, perhaps you'll be "summoned" to appear on a news program to defend, explain, or justify something that's potentially embarrassing to your organization. A sampling of crises:

• food tampering

• an airline crash

- a devastating fire

- drug abuse

- union corruption

- criminal activity

- employee layoffs

No matter whether you're "invited" or "summoned" to appear on TV—either way, you've got to come across to the viewing audience with credibility, clarity, and competence. These TV interview tips should help:

Before the interview

- *Set your objective.* Pick two or three key points you want to stress during the interview. Make them simple, powerful, and relevant.

- *Watch the program.* Observe the host's style. Is your interviewer generally friendly or antagonistic . . . pro-business or antibusiness . . . concise or long-winded . . . well-prepared or prone to wing it?

- *Ask about the format.* Length of interview? Taped or live? Other guests? Number and duration of commercials? Policy on call-ins?

- *Provide accurate information.* Make sure the producer has an accurate description of your credentials. Clarify the proper pronunciation of your name.

- *Anticipate likely questions.* The best way to do this: Put yourself in the interviewer's shoes, then imagine the questions *you'd* ask in that situation.

- *Prepare effective answers.* Be brief, be specific, be helpful. Use terms the audience will understand. Be prepared with anecdotes the audience will enjoy. Use real-life situations the audience can relate to. Practice your answers out loud, and tape-record them. Review the tapes: Cut any long parts, and spice up any dull parts.

- *Pay attention to your appearance.*   How you look will be as important as what you say, so dress appropriately for the occasion. (Again, it pays to watch the program in advance. Ask yourself: "How will my outfit look against *this* particular set?") In general, be neat and be conservative. Whatever you do, don't let your clothes overpower your message.

During the interview

- *Arrive early.*   Let's face it: TV studios can be downright overwhelming. The glaring lights, the high-tech cameras, the multiple monitors, the hustle and bustle of assistant producers, the technicians' jargon—all are potentially intimidating.

  So, don't arrive at the last minute. Give yourself a chance to look around and get familiar with all the sights and sounds. Then, you can put these distractions aside and focus on the *important* thing: To give a good interview!

- *Concentrate.*   Once the interview starts, you must give it your concentrated attention. Really *listen* to the interviewer's questions. Above all, listen for opportunities where you can reinforce your main points.

- *Be clear.*   Don't hem and haw. Don't ramble. Don't filibuster. Open your answer with a simple statement ("That's right," "No, not really," "Absolutely," "That's a common misconception," "Yes, it's true."), then add the necessary details to support your case.

- *Be human.*   Tell a personal story. Give a quick case history. Share a recent example. Use a lively quotation or a revealing anecdote. Tap into the emotions of the audience.

All of these techniques will help you come across as a believable, trustworthy, and caring individual.

- *Be conversational.* Leave your jargon back at your office. Keep your boring statistics locked in your briefcase.

- *Be helpful.* Try to approach the topic from the audience's perspective. Give examples they can relate to. Offer solutions they can put into practice.

- *Be visual.* Television is a visual medium. If you've got terrific film footage, or relevant documents, or startling photographs, or interesting objects, use them to your advantage.

- *Use appropriate body language.* Beware of "grand movements." Sure, they might look great when you're standing at the lectern on a big stage—but when you appear on a small TV screen in someone's bedroom, those same movements can make you look downright silly. Another caution: Avoid repeatedly nodding "yes" as your interviewer asks questions. Just listen—then let your response reflect your opinion.

- *Take advantage of commercial breaks.* Use this time to collect your thoughts, to do a mental rundown, and to make sure you're getting in your basic points. Ask the host what's next—and even suggest a specific area you'd like to discuss (politely, of course).

- *Exude confidence.* After all, if *you* don't have faith in your own expertise, why should the audience?

- *Radiate charisma.* Sincerity and charm sell—and nowhere do they sell better than on TV. Remember that, and you can't go too wrong.

The Power of a Short Answer

One time, Barbara Bush made the risky comment that New York City mayor Ed Koch was "full of it."

Later, a reporter tried to grill her on this comment—wanting to know exactly what she meant, and no doubt hoping she'd stick her foot in her mouth.

With classic Barbara Bush wit, she simply smiled and gave this answer: "Joy."

Hard to do much better than that.

How to Handle Trick Questions

Questions often fall into patterns. If you recognize the pattern, you can get around the question much better.

Be aware of these trick questions:

- *The "A" or "B" Question.* "Which is more important to your company—building a new production plant in our town or opening new offices out-of-state?"

  Don't pigeonhole yourself. Say, "They're both important," or "Those are just two of our concerns."

- *The Multiple Question.* "Will the university make a special effort to recruit minority students? And will the athletic program be more closely supervised? And will you build any more student housing?"

  Don't get confused by three or four questions at once. Answer only one.

- *The Open Question.* "Tell me about your company."

  Here is where it pays off to have preestablished *focus statements*. Use them to create the image you want.

- *The "Yes" or "No" Question.* "Will you have any lay-offs next year—yes or no?"

Never get forced into a yes or no. Make the statement in your own words.

- *The Hypothetical Question.* "What if the union doesn't accept this offer?" Avoid being pulled into "doomsday" situations. They're like bottomless pits. Cut off the discussion by saying, "We're confident we'll reach an agreement." Consider this exchange from a news conference with President Reagan:

Q: "Mr. President, if there's no change in the situation, is there a time when you would want to bring the troops home?"

A: "Let me just say that—I got into trouble a little while ago from trying to answer a hypothetical question with a hypothetical answer. And various interpretations were placed on it."

Reagan then avoided a hypothetical answer and gave a *focus statement* that summed up his position.

- *The Off-the-Record Question.* There is no such thing as an off-the-record question in a Q&A session. Answer all questions as though your answer will appear on the front page of tomorrow's paper. It just might!

- *The Ranking Question.* "Would you name the top three concerns of today's teaching profession?"

    Again, don't pigeonhole yourself. As soon as you name the top three concerns, someone will ask, "What's the matter? Don't you care about (*blank*)?" Then you'll be stuck. Instead, try, "Among our most important concerns are . . ."

- *The Nonquestion Question.* "I don't think we need all this new equipment."

    How can you respond to such a statement? By converting it into a question. For example: "I'm hearing an important question in your statement, and that question is, 'How can we benefit by using this equipment?'" Then, you can answer the question without having to rebut the original statement.

- *The False Premise Question.* "Now that you've dumped all that pollution into the river, how are you going to clean it up?"

  Always correct a false premise. Say in a firm voice, "That's not so. Let me set the record straight."

- *The Cross-Examination Question.* "Let's review the waste-disposal issue once again. What possible explanation can you give for this disgraceful situation?"

  If the questioner has sneaky motives, address them. Say, "That sounds like a trap. What are you trying to get me to say?" *Remember:* You are not in a courtroom. You do not have to subject yourself to a cross-examination.

What to Include in Your Answer

- *Cite your own professional experience.* "In my twenty-five years of work in this field, I have never seen anything like that."

- *Cite your own personal experience.* "Well, I just went out and bought a (*blank*). I know the product's good."

- *Quote the experts.* "The top researchers in the country would disagree with you. At Columbia University, for example, . . ."

- *Present facts.* "The fact of the matter is . . ."

- *Disassociate.* "That's like comparing apples and avocados. We can't be compared."

- *Establish a bond.* "Well, I can certainly understand how you feel. In fact, many people have felt the same way, but when they became more familiar with the program, they found out that . . ."

- *Simplify the numbers.* "Yes, $10,000 *does* seem like a lot of money to spend on training until you consider that this amounts to only 'x' dollars per person. However, increased productivity will pay back our initial investment in just one year."

- *Recognize the importance of the question.* Some people don't want an answer. They just want to be heard. They want their day in court. If you recognize this need for attention, you will satisfy them. Play psychologist and say in your most soulful voice, "Sounds like that's an important issue to you." However, be careful not to sound patronizing.

- *Above all, include your focus statements.* Use those one-liners that will stick in the minds of the audience—and may be quoted by the press.

How to Use a Bridging Response

Use a *bridging response* when you don't want to discuss the question. Listen to the question, then bridge to one of your focus statements by saying something like this:

- "Well, Paul, the really important issue we should be discussing is . . ."

- "Consumers would be better off if they asked about . . ."

- "That's not the critical issue here. The critical issue is . . ."

In each case, use the bridging response to get into a specific point you want to make.

If possible, address the questioner by name. It produces a calming, persuasive effect.

Use Humor Sparingly—If at All

It's too easy for humor to backfire in a question-and-answer session. Why? Because it seems to be directed at a particular person. If you pick on someone whom the audience really likes, you're in trouble.

For example, "You'd better get to the point of your question because I'm only president of this organization for another eight months." Such a line might draw a laugh, but if you happen to say it to the wrong person, the audience may turn against you.

Of course, there's a flip side to this coin:

If a *questioner* says something funny, chuckle. Show you're human. Never try to top someone's line. Let that person have a brief, shining moment of glory. The audience will appreciate—and respond to—your good-naturedness.

T E N

The Nitty-Gritty Details

✳ ――――――――――――――――――――――――――――――

I never dared step into the pulpit without everything,
including the Lord's Prayer and the announcements, fully
written out in front of me.
—Frederick Buechner

――――――――――――――――――――――――――――――――――

Why worry about giving a speech? You'll be much better off if
you put your energy into thinking and planning. Think about
the logistics of giving your speech. Plan for the unexpected and
the unwanted. And prepare, prepare, prepare.

This chapter will show you how to:

- prepare *your speech* for delivery by typing the manuscript in an easy-to-read script format

- prepare *the room* by controlling the physical layout

- prepare *audiovisual materials* that work for you, not against you

HOW TO TYPE A SPEECH

Type your speech so that:

- it is easy for you to deliver

- it is easy for the press to read

• it is easy for a substitute speaker to deliver if you are unable to speak

Proper manuscript preparation takes some extra effort, but your efforts will pay off.

Here are twenty-two tips from the professionals:

1. Type the manuscript in a large-size font.

2. Use upper and lower case. DO NOT TYPE IN ALL CAPS.

3. Use a ragged right margin. Never justify the right margin.

4. Identify the speech on the top left corner of the first page with:

> your name and title
> the title of your speech
> the group you're speaking to
> the city you're speaking in
> the date of the speech

5. Double-space between lines. Triple-space between paragraphs.

6. Start typing the speech about three inches from the top of the first page. This gives you the space to make last-minute additions to your openings.

7. Be sure to end each line with a complete word. *Never* hyphenate words at thc cnds of lines. Leave the line short rather than hyphenate.

8. Don't break statistics at the end of a line. For example:

> "At our company we spend five
> hundred dollars a week on maintenance."
>   (When delivering this speech, you might accidentally say "five thousand dollars" and would have to correct yourself.)

9. End each page with a complete paragraph. It's too dangerous to start a sentence on one page and finish it on another. You can lose too much time while shifting the page.

10. Be sure to leave at least three inches of white space at the bottom of *each* page. If you try reading copy that runs all the way to the bottom of the page, your head will go too far down, the audience won't be able to see your face, and your volume will decrease.

11. Leave wide margins at the left and right of the copy.

12. Number each page on the upper right.

13. Use hyphens when you must pronounce each letter individually (for example, "M-B-A degree" or "F-A-A regulations").

14. Spell out foreign words and names phonetically. For example, after "Mr. Chianese," write "Mr. Kee-uh-NAY-zec" in parentheses.

15. Don't use roman numerals in the script. They're fine for written presentations, but not speeches. It would sound stilted to say, "now, roman numeral one . . ."

16. Underline words or phrases that are to be emphasized.

17. Use three dots (. . .) to mark slight pauses. They are often useful at the end of a paragraph, to remind you to pause for a second before proceeding.

18. Mark longer pauses with two slash marks (//). These slash marks remind you to stop for a few seconds, either to give the audience time to laugh or to give you time to change the direction of your speech. If you use slash marks, be sure to drop down a couple of lines before you start typing again. //

Like this. Otherwise, you'll obscure the marks.

19. At the end of the speech, include an address where people can write for more information.

20. Never staple the pages of your speech together. Simply fasten them with a paper clip, which can be easily removed when you're ready to speak.

21. Place the manuscript in a plain, dark folder—ready for your delivery.

22. Always prepare a spare copy and carry it separately. For example, if you're going to deliver an out-of-town speech, carry one copy in your briefcase and another in your suitcase.

Caution: None of these rules will help you much if you forget to bring the speech along—or, if you mistakenly grab another document on your way to the lectern.

In England years ago, a vice-admiral stood up to speak to the Royal Navy Old Comrades Association. After taking a careful second look at his notes, he was forced to end even before he began.

His confession to the puzzled audience? "By mistake, I brought a shopping list my wife gave me."

Tip: When people in the audience ask you to send copies of your speech, have them put their requests on the back of their business cards. You'll have completely accurate mailing information—without having to write a single word.

HOW TO PREPARE THE ROOM

It's amazing how many good speeches have been ruined by a nonfunctioning microphone or miserable lighting or a poor ventilating system.

You may have prepared a wise and witty speech, but if the audience can't hear you or see you, who cares? And if the audience is suffering from an air-conditioning system that doesn't work, you might as well wrap it up early and head home.

Check out the room before you speak. If you can't go in person, ask someone else to look at it. Or telephone the person who invited you to speak. Ask some basic questions:

- *Does the room have unwanted mirrors?* When I attended the 2002 conference of the American Society of Journalists and Authors in New York City, I watched award-winning writers make their acceptance speeches in a most unnerving setting. The hotel had placed the lectern directly in front of a huge mirror, so the audience got a rear-end view of each presenter. No speaker wants to appear in such a vulnerable and unflattering position—with nervous mannerisms on full view for all to see, and no privacy to place notes or hide a watch. Insist that a hotel either cover the offending mirror or move the lectern.

- *Does the room have windows?* Even more important, do the windows have heavy drapes? You'll need to close them if you show slides.

    You'll also need to close the drapes if you're speaking in a motel conference room that looks onto a swimming pool. There's *no way* you can compete with outdoor entertainment, so shut those drapes before the audience arrives and save yourself a lot of frustration during the speech.

- *Is there a lectern?* Does it have a light? Is it plugged in and ready to go? Is a spare bulb handy?

    Does the lectern have a shelf underneath where you can keep a glass of water, a handkerchief, a few cough drops?

    Can the lectern be adjusted to the proper height? If you're short, is there a box to stand on? Move everything into place *before* you arrive at the lectern to speak.

- *Can you be heard without a microphone?* If so, don't use one.

- *Is the public address system good?* Test it and ask an assistant to listen to you. Must you stoop or lean to reach the microphone? It should be pointed at your chin. Can you be heard in all corners of the room? Is the volume correct? Do you get feedback? Where do you turn the microphone on and off?

- *How about the lighting?* Do a "test run" with the houselights. Do they create a glare when you look at the audience? In general, the light level on you should be about the same as the light level on the audience. Does a crystal chandelier hanging over your head create a glare for the audience? Remove the bulbs. Will the spotlight appear where it should? Adjust it.

- *What about the seating?* After they've taken off their coats and seated themselves and gotten comfortable, people hate to be asked to move. Perhaps it reminds them of school days. Be sure to arrange the seating to your advantage *before* the audience arrives.

  Will people be seated at round dining tables, with some of their backs to you? If so, allow time for them to shuffle their seats before you start to speak.

  It's too difficult to maintain eye contact when listeners are scattered around a large room. If you expect a small crowd, try to remove some of the chairs before the audience arrives. Do anything you can to avoid "gaps" in the audience where energy can dissipate.

  If you'll speak in a large auditorium, have the rear seats roped off. This forces the audience to sit closer to you. This roped-off area is also great for latecomers. They can slip in without disturbing the rest of the audience.

  If only a few people show up, move your lectern from the stage to floor level to create more intimacy. The closer you are to your listeners, and the closer your listeners are to each other, the more successful you will be.

- *Is there good ventilation?* Can the air-conditioning system handle large crowds? Can the heat be regulated?
  Hotels are notoriously stuffy. One time I had to give a speech at a big hotel in New York City, and when I arrived, I found the room temperature had been set at eighty degrees. I immediately pushed the thermostat way back—and by the time the audience arrived, the room was comfortable.
  Rule: Always arrive well ahead of your audience, so you can make these necessary changes more easily.

- *How many doors lead into the room?* Can you lock the doors at the front of the room to prevent intruders from upstaging you? Can you have assistants posted at the rear doors to ensure quiet entrances from latecomers and quiet exits from people who must leave before you finish?

- *Is music being "piped" into the room?* If so, turn it off immediately. Do not rely on hotel staff to do so when it's your time to speak.

- *Is the room soundproof?* This becomes a critical issue when you speak in a hotel room. Who knows what will be happening in the room next to yours: a raucous bachelor party, a pep rally, or an enthusiastic sales pitch. What audience would concentrate on, say, cogeneration if they could listen to the excitement happening next door?
  Don't take any chances. If possible, make an unannounced visit to the hotel to check things out for yourself. Hotel managers always say their conference rooms are "nice and quiet." Trust them about as far as you could throw the hotel.
  If you find that sound carries through the walls, speak to the manager. Ask to have the adjacent rooms empty during your speech. If the hotel is booked solid,

they won't be able to accommodate this request, but it doesn't hurt to ask.

- *Where can you find help?* Get the name and telephone number of a maintenance person who can step right in and replace a fuse or a lightbulb, or adjust the air conditioner. Keep this person's name and number handy at all times.

Emerson was right. *Shallow* men believe in luck.

HOW TO USE AUDIOVISUAL AIDS

More speeches are ruined by audiovisual aids than are improved by them. I caution all speakers to be especially careful here. Don't ruin a first-rate speech with audiovisual materials that are second-rate, or even unnecessary.

A-V aids are unnecessary if they:

- contribute no new information to your speech

- fail to help the audience understand or appreciate your message

- actually *detract* from your role as speaker

Unfortunately, most speakers use audiovisual aids as a "crutch." An all-too-common example: The speaker says, "I want to tell you about our new accounting system," and then flashes a slide that reads "New Accounting System."

Does this slide contribute any new information? No. Does this slide really help the audience to understand the speaker's message? No. Does this slide detract from the speaker's presence? Unfortunately, yes.

Speeches are designed primarily for the ear, but visuals are designed for the eye. If you are trying to talk while people are looking at visual aids, rather than at you, your words won't be as powerful. Your eye contact with the audience won't be as strong. In short, your message won't be as effective.

Need convincing? Try holding an important conversation on the telephone while looking at a television show. How much information will you miss?

If you really need to use audiovisual aids—to simplify complex information or to create an emotional appeal—use them wisely.

One effective technique is to use an audiovisual "insert." Prepare a short slide show or a videotape and insert this into your speech as a self-contained unit. The audience can concentrate on the audiovisual segment and then return concentration to the remainder of your speech.

PowerPoint

> People are not listening to us, because they are spending so much time trying to understand these incredibly complex slides.
> —Army Secretary Louis Caldera

PowerPoint 1.0 went on sale in 1987—and it's safe to say, presentations haven't been the same since.

Millions of PowerPoint presentations are made every day. Military briefings, corporate presentations, college and university meetings, even church announcements—folks of all ilk now use PowerPoint without even thinking about it. And therein lies the problem.

What started out as useful presentation software has run amok. Too many people give PowerPoint presentations because—well, "because everyone else is giving them." And that's a pitiful excuse.

PowerPoint "use" has degenerated into "abuse"—with so many spinning pie charts and exploding images that the main message gets lost in a kaleidoscope of bells and whistles. Is it any wonder we see a backlash? Savvy executives now know they can distinguish themselves by appearing at a conference *without* the ubiquitous PowerPoint.

In 2000, Gen. Hugh Shelton, chairman of the Joint Chiefs of Staff, made news when he told U.S. military bases around the world to stop the escalating use of presentation software. (Apparently, all those e-mailed military briefings were taking up too much classified bandwidth.) Gen. Shelton had the guts to tackle communication's most sacred cow. I've admired the man ever since.

The truth is: The *power* is really in the *point*. No gradient-color backgrounds can compensate for poor content—and no sound effects can hide poor delivery. I counsel my clients to *ditch the PowerPoint glitz*—urging them, instead, to craft a powerful message and to polish an appealing delivery.

Too many speakers spend too much time messing around with PowerPoint production—and not enough time honing their message, or improving their delivery skills.

This overuse of presentation software has become more than a communication problem: It's a productivity problem, as well. Previously, senior executives would delegate slide production—either asking their assistants to do the job or hiring freelance artists, but no more. Today, highly paid executives waste endless hours trying to produce their own PowerPoint—only to end up with boring templates and amateurish visuals. That's not smart communication—and it's not smart business, either.

I'm reminded of that old saw, "The person who serves as his own attorney has a fool for a client." The same could be said about presenters. *The executive who serves as his own graphic designer has a fool for a client.*

If you're going to use any presentation software, use it for a reason—and use it well.

Designing a PowerPoint presentation

Everyone thinks they can design their own A-V. They can't. I know, because I've had to sit through countless PowerPoint presentations that violated the most basic design principles.

Justified right margins . . . drop shadows . . . needless fly-ins . . . endless spirals . . . pointless checkerboards . . . angled typography . . . reverse type . . . miniscule type size . . . internal capitalization . . . too much copy . . . too little white space; these are the hallmarks of ill-designed PowerPoint. They make a presentation look hokey.

If you lack talent in graphic design (and most of us do— including me), hire a talented person to design your slides. You'll save a lot of time— and wind up with a much better product.

Writing a PowerPoint presentation

What's the single most important thing you can do to write better presentations? *Use slide headlines that sell your message.* For example:

- Ditch those all-too-common one-word titles, like "Efficiency." Instead, write a benefit-oriented headline that grabs your audience: "How to Improve Efficiency in Three Steps."

- Don't settle for a bland title like "Quarterly Sales." Instead, make your headline tell the success story: "Sales Soar in Third Quarter."

- Avoid merely listing a topic, like "Environmental Costs." Instead, intrigue your audience with "Seven Environmental Costs Nobody Likes to Talk About."

Delivering a PowerPoint presentation

What's the single most important thing you can do to improve your delivery when using slides? *Maintain strong eye contact.* Don't turn away from the audience to refer to the screen. Pointing to your charts with shaky pens, quivery Laser pointers, and waggling fingers will not enhance your professionalism. It will merely give the audience a good view of your back. Trust me on this: They did not come to see your back.

Instead, direct your audience to focus on key elements by

using strong visual elements. Attract their eyes with a bold arrow, carefully boxed text, or maybe some underlining. You'll increase their comprehension—and maintain your stature as a presenter.

Here are some additional tips:

- Set written copy flush left, with a ragged right margin.

- Keep type uniform.

- Use upper- and lowercase letters.

- Limit capitalization. IF YOU INSIST ON TYPING YOUR SLIDES IN ALL CAPS, YOU WILL FORCE THE AUDIENCE TO READ SLOWER—AND YOU WILL ALSO REDUCE THEIR ABILITY TO COM-PREHEND YOUR MESSAGE. Don't make this mis-take. Limit the ALL CAPS style to headlines and occasional short phrases. Your audience will be much more comfortable when they see a natural capitalization pattern on your slides.

- Use normal spacing between words and caps.

- Keep headings uniform. Use smaller sizes on subheads to indicate relative importance.

- Use only a few lines of type on any slide.

- Use color on charts and graphs to add interest and to boost comprehension.

- Double-check everything to make sure it is in proper order.

- Everything on a slide must be visible to the people in the last row. Take a look at your visuals from the back of the room.

- Tape down cords so no one will trip.

- Leave each slide on the screen long enough for you to make your point, then move on to the next one. The audience's interest will flag if a slide is left on too long.

Video Clips

- Only use video to *reinforce* your message. Remember your eighth grade history teacher who played movies when she hadn't bothered to plan a real lesson? Don't make that mistake. Avoid "entertainment for entertainment's sake." Your video clips should *supplement* a well-planned presentation—not replace it.

- Get in, get out—maybe a minute here, or a minute there. That's why they're called video "clips." If they run too long, they're called video "distractions." Know the difference.

- Use a consistent theme and style. Multiple video clips need to share a similar look (just like the rest of your presentation shares a similar look). Don't let your audience get lost in a mishmash of clip styles.

- Pay attention to your technology. Check and adjust all equipment in advance. Have enough monitors available. The audience should not have to strain to see your video.

- Don't be afraid to use emotional appeal. Videotapes are uniquely suited to offering slice-of-life material. For example, if you're giving a speech on the need to donate blood, try a short videotape showing the people who benefit from blood donations. Get close-ups of faces, of children holding their parents' hands, and of doctors comforting patients. Don't use "perfect" people. Use "real" people who look like your audience.

Flip Charts

Remember how effectively General Norman Schwarzkopf used flip charts during the briefings for Desert Storm? No wishy-washy A-V for "Stormin' Norman."

General Schwarzkopf used neat, simple, understated flip charts. And, in doing so, he ushered in "the era of the chart" in corporate America.

Alas, while many business leaders adopted Schwarzkopf's use of flip charts, they have failed to use them as effectively as the general. Perhaps these guidelines will help:

- Use flip charts only with small groups. (What's the sense in showing a chart that can't be read beyond the third row?)

- Keep your lettering clear, bold, brief, and horizontal.

- Avoid using more than three or four curves on any graph—particularly if the curves cross one another. (Otherwise, you'll present something that resembles a splattering of spaghetti.)

- Differentiate between curves by using various thicknesses and patterns. For your most important curve, use a bold line. For the next in importance, use a light line. For the third, use a series of dashes. For the least important, use a series of dots.

- Don't turn your back to the audience when you refer to the flip charts.

- If you point out something particular on the chart, be sure you're pointing accurately. (Try to avoid the befuddled weatherman syndrome. You know what I mean— when the TV weatherman refers to a blizzard in Wisconsin, but carelessly waves his pointer somewhere around Arkansas. This is hardly a way to inspire confidence in any audience.)

- If you're going to write on your flip charts in front of the audience, make sure ahead of time that you've got several working markers. (President Reagan once got stuck with a grease pencil that failed to function. I also remember watching an otherwise competent manager grow increasingly flustered when his first marker proved dry—and the replacements proved dry, as well.)

Sound Effects

In his new role as mayor of New York City, Michael Bloomberg rang the bell at the New York Stock Exchange—and made it more than a ceremonial gesture with these words: "Since I'm probably the only mayor who was at one point in their life a member of the New York Stock Exchange, it was particularly fun to stand up there. There is nothing that is as much a symbol of New York as the New York Stock Exchange."

Each year, the Bucks County chapter of Mothers Against Drunk Driving holds a special ceremony at the county courthouse to remember the thousands who are killed and injured each year in alcohol-related crashes. Throughout the service, a bell rings every thirty seconds—representing the losses suffered throughout the United States because of drunk drivers.

Objects

Want to show off an interesting object, or hold up an unusual item, or share a powerful photo? Fine—just make sure everyone can see what you've got.

1. Lift it up in the air.
2. Hold it steady for a few moments.

3. Then, move it slowly so everyone in the room has time to see it. (Be quiet while you're moving the object. Let people look at it in silence. Otherwise, they won't be paying full attention to your words. Even worse, once the object is out of their view, they'll feel they're missing something if they continue to hear you explaining the item.)

Creative Props

In a State of the Union address, President Ronald Reagan once held up forty-three pounds of federal budget documents for everyone to eyeball, then dropped them to the floor with a dramatic thud—promising he'd never approve any such budget.

When Senator Alfonse D'Amato spoke about high taxes during a budget debate, he provided a drawing of the dreaded "Taxasaurus monster," which he then stabbed by using an oversize pencil—all the while shouting, "Kill the monster, kill him now."

When Mark Gearan was named communications director in the Clinton White House, he brought along his wife and fourteen-month-old daughter to the announcement. While the cameras clicked happily away, Gearan looked at his baby and quipped, "Any prop I can get."

Also, who could ever forget the spectacle of that rifle being waved at the Waco hearings in the U.S. Capitol? Of course, your props don't have to be quite so extreme.

Lt. Col. James "Mike" McAlister, U.S. Army, offers this wonderful suggestion for creating a very simple, but memorable, prop. When his commanding general is asked to preside at a special ceremony (to promote someone or present an award), McAlister makes a list of things that people admire about the honoree and puts this list on a 5" × 7" card. The comments are short, friendly, and upbeat ("goes out of his way to help people"; "love the man even after he chewed me out," and "this is the one guy I want beside me when all hell breaks loose"). After the commanding general reads these praises in front of the assembled audience, he then hands the 5" × 7" card directly to the honoree as a keepsake. Great idea, Lieutenant Colonel McAlister!

Emergency A-V Kit

If you plan to give a computer presentation, be realistic. Ask yourself, "What if I couldn't get an Internet connection right away? What if my computer wouldn't work?"

Prepare carefully—but realize: Even with careful preparation, things can go wrong when you use A-V. As a general rule, the more sophisticated the A-V, the more complex the problems. In reality, a multimedia presentation poses a whole lot more risks than a flip chart.

Carry an emergency kit to all presentations. Include:

- a second hard drive
- extension cords
- spare lightbulbs
- three-pronged adapters
- a multiple-outlet box
- masking tape
- scissors
- screwdriver
- pliers
- a small flashlight

After all, a speech that cost thousands to prepare can be ruined by the failure of a $1.19 lightbulb. Prevent failure. Prepare carefully.

Copyright Issues

If you think you'd like to:

- play the CD of an inspirational song during your award ceremony

- include some clever political cartoons in your next slide presentation

- show excerpts of a popular movie at a company employee meeting

- photocopy magazine articles to use as handouts

- reproduce artwork as illustrations for your presentation

- combine articles to use as a "course-pack" for your next training session

- photocopy parts of a book that your audience might find useful

Then think again.

U.S. copyright law protects the creator of the work. You cannot use that work (in any way) without the creator's permission—period. It is the creator's property, and the creator has the right to: first, control its use, and second, charge for its use.

If you find yourself thinking:

- "It's just a small audience, so copyright doesn't matter."

- "We're just a nonprofit organization. We don't have to pay any reprint fees, right?"

- "Hey, who will ever find out if I show an excerpt of this movie at my meeting?"

- "We've always photocopied articles to give as handouts at our PTA meetings."

If you're thinking anything like this—think again.

Copyright applies from the moment of creation, and you cannot use that work without permission—no ifs, ands, or buts.

So, get permission. Make sure everything is clear regarding intellectual property and copyright. Do you own the footage yourself? Then get a signed release from anyone who is captured on your video.

Do you have questions? Ask an attorney.

HOW TO PREPARE YOURSELF

When you give a speech, you want to look and sound your best. Don't leave these things to chance.

How to Look Your Best

Sometimes, the smallest clothing choice will make the biggest difference. When he hosted the historic meeting of Yasser Arafat and Yitzak Rubin on the South Lawn of the White House in 1993, President Clinton realized there were many things he couldn't control about that day—but one thing he could control was his tie. Clinton symbolically chose a tie with little trumpets on it—to trumpet the glory of Mr. Arafat and Mr. Rabin shaking hands at the accord.

Of course, not all speaking engagements are so monumental. Here are some general guidelines.

Don't wear brand-new clothes to give a speech. New clothes haven't had a chance to "fit" your body. They often feel stiff and uncomfortable, and what could be worse than having a button pop off or a seam rip open when you gesture in the middle of your speech? Wear "old favorites" instead—clothes that fit well and move the way *you* move.

Dress conservatively for most business functions. If in doubt about the suitability of a piece of clothing, don't wear it. Your appearance should not interfere with your message.

For men:

- A dark suit—clean and well-pressed, of course. (Navy blue or "banker's" blue is generally a color that conveys authority and elicits trust.)
- A long-sleeved shirt. (White or blue look best under bright lights.)
- A conservative tie with a touch of red for power (an old politician's trick)
- Long, dark socks. (The audience shouldn't see a patch of hairy leg when you sit down and cross your legs.)
- Well-shined shoes
- No pens sticking out of your shirt pocket, please
- No coins or keys bulging in your pants pockets

For women:

- A suit or a dress (static-free and noncling, of course)
- No low necklines
- Be especially careful with your hemline if you will be seated on stage before you speak.
- Moderate heels—no spiked heels that will clomp as you cross a wooden floor
- No rattling jewelry
- Arrange to leave your purse with someone in the audience. (Do not carry it to the podium.)

How to Sound Your Best

Treat your voice well. No cheering for the local football team the day before.

Ask your doctor about using a humidifier the night before. If you're staying in a hotel room, fill the bathtub with water before going to sleep. Moisture in the air will help prevent a dry-throat feeling.

Hot tea with honey and lemon is great for the voice. Use herbal tea for an extra calming effect. Chamomile tea can be particularly relaxing.

Avoid carbonated beverages prior to speaking—and surely, I shouldn't have to tell you: No alcohol.

Delivery

❋ ──────────────────────────────────

Sincerity is everything. If you can fake that, you've got it
made.
　—Comedian George Burns

──────────────────────────────────

Practice makes perfect, the saying goes. Well, practice may not
make you a perfect speaker, but it will certainly make you a
better speaker. With the right coaching, you may even become
a great speaker.

This chapter will coach you on:

- rehearsals

- executive presence

- voice control

- eye contact

- body language

It will also show you how to deal with two special concerns: nervousness and hecklers.

PRACTICING YOUR DELIVERY

Practice your *delivery*, not just your speech. It's not enough to know the *content* of your speech. You must also be comfortable with the gestures and pauses and emphases that will help get your message across to the audience.

To do this, practice the speech in six stages. First, familiarize yourself with the script itself. Then familiarize yourself with the delivery techniques you'll need.

1. *Begin by reading the speech aloud to yourself.* Tape-record it. How long does it take? Where do you need to pause to avoid running out of breath in mid-sentence? Should you rewrite any sentences so they're easier to deliver? Do you need to vary your pace?

   How does your voice sound? Does it fade at the end of sentences?

   If you generally have trouble projecting your voice, try putting the tape recorder across the room while you practice. This trick should *force* you to speak louder.

2. *Deliver the speech standing in front of a mirror.* By now, you should be familiar enough with the material to look up from the manuscript fairly often. Concentrate on emphasizing the right parts. See how your face becomes more animated at certain points in the speech.

   Caution: Be sure to rehearse the entire speech each time you practice. Otherwise, you'll have a well-prepared beginning but a weak ending.

   Deny yourself the luxury of "backtracking." If you make a mistake during rehearsal—trip on a line or leave something out—don't go back and start again. Be realistic. How would you recover from a mistake in front of an audience? That's how you should recover from it during your rehearsal.

3. *Deliver the speech to a friend.* Try to simulate a realistic environment. Stand up. Use a lectern. Arrange some chairs.

   If you need to put on glasses to see the script, now's the time to practice doing that unobtrusively. Practice moving the pages quietly to the side. Don't "flip" them over. Look at your listener.

   By this point, you should have memorized the first thirty seconds of your speech and the last thirty seconds, moments when eye contact is most critical. Do *not* try to memorize the rest of the speech, or your delivery will sound stilted. Focus on the ideas, not the words. Just look up a lot to make sure you're getting those ideas across. It's this *eye contact* with an audience that animates a speaker.

   Allow yourself to smile when it feels natural. Gesture with your hand to make a point. Let your face talk, too.

4. *Practice again before a small group.* Try to make good eye contact with each person. Play with your voice a little bit to keep your listeners' attention. Notice where it helps to speak faster, slower, louder, softer.

5. *Give it your best shot.* Consider this advice from Lord Chesterfield: "Aim at perfection in everything, though in most things it is unattainable. However, they who aim at it and persevere, will come much nearer to it than those whose laziness and despondency make them give it up as unattainable."

6. *If possible, practice on-site.* You'll feel more confident in a room that seems familiar. If you can't practice on-site, be sure to arrive extra early so you can get comfortable with the layout of the room before you begin your speech.

PRESENCE

A speech doesn't start when you begin to speak. It starts the moment you enter the room.

An audience will start to form an opinion of you as soon as they see you. First impressions count. Make yours good.

Carry yourself with presence from the moment you arrive. Be well-groomed. Don't carry loose papers. Walk in a brisk, businesslike manner. Be polite to receptionists and secretaries. They may tell their bosses about you later. It's fruitless to talk to an audience about corporate ethics if they've heard you be rude to the receptionist.

Listen carefully to other speakers and respond appropriately. Pay particular attention to the person who introduces you.

All eyes will be on you as you walk to the podium, so don't button your jacket or sort your papers. Take care of those details *before* you leave your chair.

Don't bother to hide the fact that you'll use a written text. Just carry the speech at your side— not in front of your chest, where it looks like a protective shield. If you plan to shake hands with the person who introduced you, carry the speech in your left hand so you don't have to make a last-minute switch.

Never place your speech on the lectern in advance. Someone speaking ahead of you might carry it away accidentally, and then you'd be stuck.

When you get to the lectern, take care of "The Big Seven"—preparations you can't afford to skip.

1. Open your folder and remove the paper clip from your speech.

2. Make sure the lectern is at a comfortable level. You should, of course, have adjusted it in advance, but if another speaker has changed the height, now's the time to correct it.

3. Check the position of the microphone. Again, you should have tested the microphone in advance. Check

the switch. If you question the level, just say, "Testing." *Do not blow into the microphone or tap it.*

4. Stand straight and place your weight evenly over both feet. This will help you feel "grounded" and in control of the situation.

5. Take ownership of the space. Mentally *own* that room—every inch of it.

6. *Look* at the audience before you start to speak. This pause will quiet them and give you a chance to . . .

7. . . . Breathe!
   Now, you're ready to speak.

VOICE

Demosthenes, the Athenian orator, supposedly practiced speaking with a mouthful of pebbles. You don't have to go to such extremes. When Southern-born actress Reese Witherspoon needed to prepare a British accent for *The Importance of Being Ernest,* which premiered in 2002, she practiced her voice by ordering coffee at Starbucks.

No matter where you choose to rehearse your speech, check these basics:

- *Rate.* Time yourself with a stopwatch. How many words do you speak in a minute? Most people speak about 120–150 words per minute.

- *Variety.* Can you adjust your pace? Slower to set a particular mood? Faster to create excitement?

- *Emphasis.* Do you emphasize the *right* words?

- *Volume.* Can people hear you? If not, open your mouth more.

- *Rhythm.* Do you vary your sentences?

- *Fillers*. Do you bother your listeners with "uh" and "er" and "ah"?

- *Clarity*. Do you articulate clearly? Don't slur your contractions (*wu'nt* for *wouldn't*). Don't reverse sounds (*per*scription for *pre*-scription). Don't omit sounds (lis*t*s). Don't add sounds (acros*t*).

It's Not What You Say, It's How You Say It (St. Martin's Press, 2000) offers an extensive section on vocal techniques and other delivery issues. If you're serious about improving your presentation skills, that information will prove invaluable for you.

If you have serious speech problems, I urge you to get professional help—the sooner, the better. Ask your doctor to recommend a speech therapist, or contact local colleges and universities for speech clinics. It might be the single most important investment you ever make in yourself. Good luck!

EYE CONTACT

Good eye contact will do more to help your delivery than anything else.

When you *look* at people, they believe you care about them. They believe you are sincere. They believe you are honest. How can you go wrong if an audience feels this way about you?

Really *look* at the people in your audience—and look at them as *individuals*. Don't look over their heads or stare at some vague spot in the back of the room. Don't "sweep" the room with your eyes. Instead, look directly at one person until you finish a thought, then move on to another. You must maintain good eye contact with the audience if you are going to convey sincerity.

Avoid looking repeatedly at the same person. It's best to look at as many individuals as possible in the time allowed.

Eye contact will also give you instantaneous feedback. Does the audience look interested or are they nodding out? If you sense boredom, intensify your eye contact, vary your voice, use body language.

Try not to look around the audience during grammatical pauses (for example, between sentences) because physical movement seems awkward when there's nothing verbal going on.

LECTERNS

Something as basic as using (or not using) a lectern will send a powerful signal to your audience. Most speakers use lecterns most of the time. That's reasonable. After all, lecterns provide a convenient place to put your notes and a glass of water.

Unfortunately, many speakers automatically use lecterns all of the time, and that's too bad. A lectern hides about 70 percent of your body and puts a barrier between you and your audience. Few presentations are improved by barriers.

If you're willing to step away from the lectern (even briefly), you will convey confidence, appear more likable, and become more persuasive. Isn't that worth trying?

In his official farewell address as mayor of New York City, Rudolph Giuliani stepped away from the lectern at St. Paul's Chapel and walked toward his audience—conveying a deep sense of affection for the people, and eliciting their strong support.

BODY LANGUAGE

Most books on public speaking talk about the importance of gestures. I prefer to talk about the importance of *body language*. It is, of course, important to gesture with your hands if you want to make a point. But it's just as important to speak *with your whole body*.

A raised eyebrow, a smile, a shrug of the shoulders—they all make a statement. If you use them wisely, they can contribute a lot to your speech.

If you watched TV during Operation Desert Shield and Desert Storm, you could learn a number of things about effective delivery from General H. Norman Schwarzkopf. Remember those powerful briefing sessions?

- He stood tall—generally *beside* the lectern (in contrast to many corporate speakers, who hide behind their lecterns for dear life).

- He made bold gestures, and he made them away from the body—easy for all to see.

- He kept direct eye contact with the audience.

- And—refreshing in a military authority!—he used facial expressions to convey a wide variety of emotions: determination, sympathy, pride, anger, and commitment. (No stone-faced bureaucrat, here.)

It's not necessary (or even advisable) to choreograph your body movements in advance. You'll find that they spring naturally from your message, from your belief in what you're saying. If you put energy and thought and life into your message, your body movements will take good care of themselves. If you *don't*, no amount of hand-waving will help your cause.

As you rehearse and deliver your speech:

- You'll find yourself leaning forward slightly to make a stronger point.

- You'll find yourself smiling when you quote something amusing.

- You'll find yourself nodding slightly when you sense a good response from the audience.

- You'll find yourself shaking your head when you cite something that's offensive or inaccurate.

You'll find yourself, in short, developing charisma. The more energy you *give* to an audience, the more charisma you will develop. It's an exchange—you give and you get.

A word of caution about gestures. No feeble ones, please. If you raise just a finger to make a point, the audience may not even see the gesture. Raise your whole hand. Raise your whole arm. Make your movements *say* something.

If you have trouble expressing yourself physically, swing your arms in figure-eights before you speak. (In privacy, of course.) This big movement will loosen you up.

WHEN YOU FINISH SPEAKING

You've just spoken the last word of your speech. *Be careful.* Your speech isn't really over. Don't walk away from the podium yet. Hold your position. Look directly at the audience for a few more seconds. Remain in control of the silence just as you remained in control of the speech.

If you wrote a good speech, your final words were strong and memorable. In fact, your ending was probably the best part of the whole speech. Allow it to sink in.

Then, close your folder and walk away from the podium. Walk briskly and confidently—the same way you approached the podium.

When you take your seat, do *not* start talking to the person next to you. Someone else is probably at the podium now, and the audience would think it rude for you to be talking.

Above all, don't say things like, "Whew, am I glad *that's* over," or "Could you see how much my hands were trembling?" I have even seen speakers sit down and roll their eyes and shake their heads—a sure way to detract from an otherwise good speech.

Just sit quietly. Look attentive and confident.

There may well be applause. Smile and look pleased to be there. It would seem unnatural to act any other way.

Some speakers—those with a lot at stake—even plan their

applause. They make sure that staff members attend the speech—not sitting together, but spread throughout the audience. When these people start to applaud, they produce a ripple effect. *Voilà!* A standing ovation!

NERVOUSNESS

"I'm afraid I'll be nervous." That's a common feeling, and in some ways it's healthy. It shows you care about getting your message across to the audience. You really *do* want to look and sound good.

But it's important to understand what nervousness is. Nervousness is simply *energy.* If you channel that energy, you can turn it into a positive force. You can make it work for you. You can use the extra energy to your advantage.

But if you allow that energy to go unchecked—if you allow *it* to control *you*—then you're going to have problems. A dry mouth, perhaps, or a cracking voice. Lots of rocking back and forth on your feet, or lots of "uh's" and "um's." Maybe even forgetfulness.

How can you channel your nervous energy?

By taking the advice that appears in this chapter. Learn to direct your extra energy into eye contact, body language, and vocal enthusiasm. These physical activities provide an outlet for your nervousness. They offer a way to use up some of that extra energy.

What's more, good eye contact, strong body language, and vocal enthusiasm will build your *confidence*. It's hard to feel insecure when you look directly at your listeners and see the responsiveness in their faces.

Prespeech Tricks to Prevent Nervousness

There are tricks to every trade, and public speaking is no exception. Consult with your doctor. Consider what professional speakers do to keep their nervousness in check.

• *Try physical exercises.*   Just before you speak, go off by yourself (to the restroom or to a quiet corner) and concentrate on the part of your body that feels most tense. Your face? Your hands? Your stomach? Deliberately tighten that part even more, then let go. You will feel an enormous sense of relief. Repeat this a few times.

Drop your head. Let your cheek muscles go loose and let your mouth go slack.

Make funny faces. Puff up your cheeks, then let the air escape. Or open your mouth and your eyes wide, then close them tightly. Alternate a few times.

Yawn a few times to loosen your jaw and your mucous membranes.

Pretend you're an opera singer. Try "mi, mi, mi" a few times. Wave your arms as you do it.

• *Try mental exercises.*   Picture something that's given you pleasant memories: Sailing on a blue-green ocean; swimming in a mountain lake; or walking on a beach and feeling the sand between your toes. (Water often has a calming effect on people.)

• *Try a rational approach.*   Say to yourself, "I'm prepared. I know what I'm talking about." Or, "I've spent a year working on this project. Nobody knows as much about this project as I do." Or, "I'm glad I can talk to these people. It will help my career."

I know someone who repeats to herself, "This is better than death, this is better than death." That may sound extreme, but it works for her—and, she's right. Giving a speech *is* better than death.

If you're scared to give a speech, try to think of something that's *really* frightening. The speech should seem appealing by comparison.

• *Try a test run.*   Visualize exactly what will happen after you're introduced. You'll get out of your chair;

you'll hold the folder in your left hand; you'll walk confidently across the stage; you'll hold your head high; you'll look directly at the person who introduced you; you'll shake his or her hand; you'll . . .

If you see yourself as confident and successful in your mental test run, you'll be confident and successful in your delivery.

Above all, never *say* that you're nervous. If you do, you'll make yourself more nervous, and you'll make the audience nervous, too.

During-the-Speech Tricks to Overcome Nervousness

Okay. You've prepared your speech carefully. You've done the prespeech exercises. Now you're at the podium and—can that be?—your mouth goes a little dry.

Don't panic. Just intensify your eye contact. Looking at the audience will take away your self-preoccupation and reduce the dryness.

Persistent dryness? Help yourself to the glass of water that you've wisely placed at the lectern. Don't be embarrassed. Say to yourself, "It's my speech, and I can damned well drink water if I want to."

Other minitraumas?

- *Sweat rolling off your forehead.* Wipe it away with the big cotton handkerchief that you also placed at the lectern. Don't hesitate to really *wipe*. Little dabs are ineffectual, and you'll have to dab repeatedly. Do it right the first time, and get it over with. Also, avoid using tissues. They can shred and get stuck on your face—not a terribly impressive sight.

- *A quavery voice.* Again, intensify your eye contact. Focus on *them*. Then lower your pitch and control your breath as you begin to speak. Concentrate on speaking distinctly and slowly.

• *Shaking hands.* Take heart. The audience probably can't see your trembling hands, but if they're distracting you, then use some body movement to diffuse that nervous energy. Change your foot position. Lean forward to make a point. Move your arms. (If your body is in a frozen position, your shaking will only grow worse.)

• *A pounding heart.* No, the audience *cannot* see the rising and falling of your chest. If you have concerns, ask your doctor.

• *Throat clearing.* If you have to cough, cough—away from the microphone. Drink some water, or pop a piece of a cough drop into your mouth. Again, the well-prepared speaker has an unwrapped cough drop handy at all times—and ready to use.

• *Runny nose, watery eyes.* Bright lights can trigger these responses. Simply pause, say "Excuse me," blow your nose or wipe your eyes, and get on with it. Don't make a big deal over it by apologizing. A simple "Excuse me" is just fine.

• *Nausea.* You come down with a viral infection the day before your speech and you're afraid of throwing up in the middle of it. Don't worry needlessly. Ask your doctor for advice.

For actors, the show must always go on—even with serious viral infections. More than one actor has placed a trash can backstage so he could throw up between acts. But *you* are not an actor, and you really don't have to put yourself through this test of willpower. If you are terribly ill—as opposed to being just mildly nervous—cancel your engagement. Since you've prepared a complete manuscript, perhaps a colleague could substitute for you. If substitution is not possible, offer to speak at a later date.

- *Burping.* Some people feel they have to burp when they get nervous. If you are one of these people, do plenty of physical relaxation exercises before you speak. Don't drink any carbonated beverages that day, and eat only a light lunch. Keep lunch quiet by eating alone.

- *Fumbled words.* Professional speakers, radio announcers, and television anchors fumble words fairly often. Someone once introduced President Reagan with this slip of the tongue: "Everyone who is for abortion was at one time a feces [sic]." So, why should *you* expect to be perfect?

  If it's a minor fumble, just ignore it and keep going. If it's a big one, fix it. Simply repeat the correct word—with a smile, to show you're human.

  Continue with your speech, but slow down a little bit. Once you've had a slip of the tongue, chances are high you'll have another. A fumble is a sort of symptom that you're focusing more on yourself than on your message. Relax and slow down.

- *Forgetfulness.* Some people look at an audience and forget what they want to say. Aren't you glad you made the effort to prepare a good written manuscript? It's all right there, so you have one less thing to worry about.

HECKLERS

> As a goose is not frightened by cackling nor a sheep by
> bleating, so do not let the clamor of a senseless multitude
> alarm you.
> —Epictetus

Hecklers tend to exist only in the bad dreams of speakers. They almost never pose real-life problems. However, if you are in the middle of your speech and you see someone waving an arm at you, then you need real-life help—and fast.

First of all, stay calm. Hecklers are like people who make obscene telephone calls. They just love to upset you. If you stay calm, you destroy their pleasure. If you stay calm, you also stay in control.

Ignore the hand that's waving in the air and keep right on speaking. It takes a lot of energy to wave a hand in the air, and the person will probably grow tired and give up. (Try waving your hand in the air for a few minutes, and you'll see what I mean.)

If you hear a voice? Stop speaking, remain calm, and ask the person to hold the question until after your speech. Be polite but firm. The audience will respect your approach and the person will most likely respect your request. Proceed with your speech.

If the person gets louder, you should *not* continue. Look instead at the person who organized this speaking engagement. If you're lucky, that person will come to your aid and quiet the heckler or escort him out of the room.

If not, speak to the heckler again. Say, "As I said before, I'll be glad to answer all questions *after* my speech." By now, your patience and professionalism should have earned the respect—and sympathy—of the rest of the audience.

If the heckling worsens, confront the person. Say, "Everyone here knows I'm (*name*) and I'm from the (*name*) company. Could you tell us who *you* are?" Hecklers, like obscene phone callers, prefer to remain anonymous.

If the tirade continues, you will have to count on the audience for their support. Stop speaking, and step back from the podium. Let *them* put pressure on the heckler to shut up or leave.

After all, *you* are the invited speaker, not the heckler. You shouldn't have to justify your presence. You have a right to be treated fairly and to get your message across. If the audience isn't willing to support your basic rights, then don't waste your time trying to speak to them. Leave—with dignity.

Whatever you do, try to avoid the response that Washington mayor Marion Barry made when faced with hecklers at a neighborhood festival. The embattled D.C. mayor simply shot back with an obscene gesture—hardly the way to create an image of leadership.

EMBARRASSING GLITCHES

When reviewing your speech manuscript, pay special attention to noun/verb confusions. Certain words can serve either as a noun or a verb—depending on which syllable you stress.

Consider: *produce, project, reject,* and *console.* When you put the emphasis on the first syllable, they're all nouns. ("We'll need three months to complete this project.") If you accent the second syllable, those same words become verbs. ("Here's how we project our expenses.")

If you mistakenly accent the wrong syllable, you'll look like you're "reading" your speech for the first time—which seriously undercuts your authority as a speaker. Rehearse.

TWELVE

Media Coverage

✳ ──

Looking at yourself through the media is like looking at
one of those rippled mirrors in an amusement park.
—Edmund S. Muskie, U.S. secretary of state

──

Your speech probably won't merit coverage on network television news, but there are lots of other ways to get good publicity
for your speech.

Start small and work your way up the publicity scale.
Begin with the basics and do as much as your budget and your
time will allow—and, yes, as much as your *material* will allow.

Face it. Not all speeches are newsworthy. If you expect the
media to pay attention to a routine speech, you will be disappointed.

Here are nine ways to get good publicity for your speech:

1. *Give it a catchy title.*   Come up with titles that *beg* to
   be quoted.

   Need ideas? Try variations on the titles of popular
   movies, books, and songs. Be specific. Be graphic. Be
   irreverent if you want. Just don't be boring.

   Consider these examples:

   • "Advice from an S.O.B.: Thrive or Die" (by Allen
   Neuharth, Gannett Foundation, to Society of Professional Journalists)

- "When Will It Be Fun to Fly Again?" (by Robert Aaronson, Air Transport Association, at British-American Business Association)

- "Make a Difference Instead of a Deal" (by David Tappan, Jr., Fluor Corporation, at University of Southern California Graduate School of Business)

- "To Be or Not to Be: The Hamlet Syndrome in Canada" (by R. D. Fullerton, Canadian Imperial Bank of Commerce, at Vancouver Board of Trade)

- "What Would You Do If *Your* Name Were on the Building?" (by Melvin Goodes, Warner-Lambert Company, at Strategic Planning Conference)

  Avoid titles that sound like doctoral dissertations (e.g., "The Inherent Challenges of Economic Redistribution in the 21st century"). Nobody wants to quote anything that sounds like a textbook.

2. *Distribute copies to the audience.* Always do this *after* your presentation, not before. Otherwise, they'll be reading and rustling papers while you're trying to speak.

   One good way: Have assistants at the doors as the audience leaves.

3. *Give a copy to your employee information staff.* Your public relations department may post the speech on their Web site or plan a related story for the employee newspaper.

4. *Send an advance copy of the speech to the trade publication that serves your business.* Make the editor's work easier:

- Be sure the speech is easy to read—with short paragraphs and wide margins. (See chapter 10 for details.) Add subheads to catch the editor's attention.

- Use colored ink to underline a couple of quotable phrases in the speech—phrases the editor can pull out and use in a caption or headline or call-out.

- Attach a one-page summary. This summary may be the only thing the editor bothers to read, so make it good.

- Highlight the speech's main points. Include an impressive statistic or a memorable quote or an interesting example—anything to grab the editor's attention.

5. *Send a copy to nearby colleges and universities.*

- The placement office may want to file your speech and share it with students who apply to your company.

- The appropriate department may want to present your ideas in class.

- The campus newspaper may want to cover your speech, especially if its content affects the lives of students.

6. *Prepare news releases for newspapers and local radio or TV stations.*   Make your releases short and snappy. Don't think "corporate." Think "newsworthy, interesting, or important." Put yourself in the shoes of an editor or a news director and ask, "What kind of press release would I like to receive?" The universal answer: "The kind of press release that makes my work easier."

   For newspapers: Give them a good lead, something they can use "as is." Editors aren't looking for more work. They're looking for good stories to make their work easier. Give them a good lead, and they may give you good coverage.

   For radio and TV: Give them three or four short sentences written for the ear and ready to deliver on the air. Remember: News directors receive many press releases each day. It's human nature for them to use the ones that are "ready to go"—that don't require extensive research and rewriting.

7. *Appear on a radio or TV interview program.* How can you get booked for an interview program? Call the station about two weeks in advance and let the program director know why the story is newsworthy. Be brief. Program directors have busy schedules and won't listen to a long-winded pitch.

   If you sense interest, offer written backup material. Include any recent publications. A book or a magazine feature will increase your credibility. For TV shows, offer to provide visuals—slides, film footage, small-scale models, even documents to lift and show as you make your point.

   Television is a highly visual medium. If you offer to show things to the viewers, you will stand a better chance of getting on the show.

8. *Reprint the speech and take a direct-mail approach.* If your budget allows, you might want to publish a booklet with a bold cover. Be sure to consider postage costs when you design your reprints.

9. *Submit a copy to:*

- *The Executive Speaker*
  P.O. Box 292437
  Dayton, OH 45429
  mail@executive-speaker.com
  This monthly publication reprints excerpts of speeches on a wide variety of topics. It also serves as a national clearinghouse for business speeches and keeps thousands of noteworthy speeches on file in its library. Inclusion in this publication can bring your speech to the attention of people in many organizations around the country.

- *Vital Speeches*
  389 Johnnie Dodd Blvd.
  Box 1247
  Mount Pleasant, SC 29465
  vitalspeeches@awod.com
  This biweekly publication reprints entire manuscripts of significant speeches. The front cover reads, "The best thought by the best minds on current issues"—and the list of contributors reads like a who's who in international politics and business. This prestigious forum has a tough selection process, but if you've produced a particularly well-written speech on a noteworthy topic, you'll want to make the extra effort to send *Vital Speeches* a copy. I've been able to get considerable attention for my clients through this publication, and I would urge you to consider it as a valuable public relations and marketing tool.

Make the most of your speech. After all, you worked hard to prepare it. Now, make it work hard for *you*.

THIRTEEN

International Speeches

✳ ─────────────────────────────────────

Az me kunt iber di planken, bakumt men andereh gedanken.
[If you cross over the fence, you acquire other ideas.]
—Yiddish proverb

─────────────────────────────────────

The globalization of business has brought many changes—not the least of which is a critical need to "cross over the fence" and communicate with international audiences.

An American manufacturer has to give a speech in Moscow, Japanese executives must give an important presentation in California, a German banker needs to address a group of international bankers in London, Mexican leaders want to talk about trade agreements with Canadian executives—these are all common assignments in today's global marketplace.

Unfortunately, few speakers have adequate experience with international audiences, and they bring many anxieties to the podium:

- How can I meet the distinctive demands of this foreign audience?

- How can I be sure my message is "getting across"?

- How can I use translators effectively?

- How can I avoid the pitfalls of cross-cultural gaffes?

- How can I use humor effectively?

- How can I show respect for my foreign hosts?

- How can I show pride in my own cultural heritage?

The following examples will show how other leaders have dealt with international speaking assignments. Perhaps you can gain some ideas by listening to their techniques.

HOW TO GET YOUR MESSAGE ACROSS IN ANY LANGUAGE

Make It Timely

When former president Jimmy Carter delivered a speech at the University of Havana in 2002, he gained media attention as the first U.S. president to visit Cuba since Castro took power back in 1959.

Speaking in Spanish using a prepared text, Carter broke through four decades of mistrust with these words: "It is time for us to change our relationship and the way we think and talk about each other."

Express Your Pleasure at the Privilege of Addressing This Foreign Audience

As the chairman of the Fiat Group, Giovanni Agnelli was asked to give the annual Romanes Lecture at Oxford University in England. He acknowledged the cross-cultural honor this way:

> Over the past hundred years, the Romanes Lecture has been given by some of Britain's most illustrious men and women. I believe this is the first time that an Italian has been invited to take the platform at this

prestigious event, and I am most grateful to the chancellor and the University of Oxford authorities for according me the honour.

However, I should perhaps warn you that I am an industrialist, *not* an academic, and so I hope you will not expect me to give you a lecture in the strict sense of the word.

What I would like to do instead is to discuss a subject currently of major public interest: *What is Europe?*

Include References to Your Own Cultural Values

When the emir of Kuwait spoke before a United Nations General Assembly, he opened by giving a short Moslem prayer. And he ended with these moving words:

> The State of Kuwait will remain, as always, faithful to its principles, true to its system of values, close to its friends, and respectful of its obligations and commitments.
>
> Together, we will join hands in concert and harmony to secure our development and progress. This will be a fulfillment of God's promise as rendered in the following verse:

> > O ye who believe,
> > If you will aid [the cause of]
> > Allah, He will aid you,
> > And plant your feet firmly.
> > (*Koran* 47:7)

> And whose word can be truer than Allah's?
> Thank you and may Allah, our Lord, bring you all peace and grace.

Use a Quotation That Reflects Your Host Country's Culture

When Vicente Fox, president of the United Mexican States, spoke before a Joint Session of Congress in 2001, he concluded with this quote by President John F. Kennedy: "We stand today on the edge of a New Frontier . . . the New Frontier of which I speak is not a set of promises—it is a set of challenges."

Be Vivid

When newly elected Brazilian president Fernando Collor de Mello evaluated the economic situation in his country, he used highly visual details that would make a powerful impression in *any* language:

> I am driving a packed bus at 150 kilometers per hour, headed for a cliff. Either we put on the brakes and some people get a little bruised up, or we go over the edge and we all die.

Be Inclusive

When President George W. Bush spoke at the Summit of the Americas in Quebec, he reached out to all the leaders of the hemisphere's democracies with these international examples:

- Champlain sailing the Caribbean, as well as the St. Lawrence
- a quotation by José Martí, "La libertad no es nogociable." ("Liberty is not negotiable.")
- high-paying jobs "from the Yukon to the Yucatan"

Cite Long-standing Friendships

When Abdullah II, His Majesty, king of Jordan, spoke to the Houses of Parliament of the United Kingdom of Great Britain and Northern Ireland, he was the first head of state from the Arab Middle East to address those parliamentary members. He began by recalling his late father, His Majesty King Hussein, who "led the way as a peace-maker and voice of moderation in the Middle East. I am delighted to see so many of his friends here today."

Emphasize the Role of Families

When first lady Laura Bush spoke about Mid-East violence at a conference in Paris in 2002, she emphasized the desire of all parents ("no matter what our differences in culture or custom or faith") to protect our children from poverty and violence:

"Every parent, every teacher, every leader has a responsibility . . ."

HOW TO USE A TRANSLATOR

> If I want to sell you something, then I speak in your language.
> Aber wenn Sie mir 'was verkaufen wollen, dann sollen Sie
> mein Sprache können. (But when you want to sell me some-
> thing, then you ought to be able to speak my language.)
> —Helmut Kohl, former chancellor of Germany

When Joseph Pulitzer published the *World* at the turn of the century, he got the bizarre idea to take his advertising campaign beyond the *earth* and extend it to the entire *universe*. How? By erecting an enormous advertising sign in New Jersey that would be visible on Mars. He abandoned his plan only when an associate asked, "What language would we print it in?"

What language, indeed?

Of course, most translation assignments prove a little more mundane than Mr. Pulitzer's, but ordinary interpretation is demanding nonetheless.

After all, there's a huge difference between someone who happens to speak a foreign language—and someone who has the highly developed skills to serve as an interpreter in important business dealings!

The former is an amateur—the latter is a professional. Business translation clearly demands a professional—and you will get only what you pay for.

If *you* are giving a speech to an audience that speaks another language, how can you find a translator who's adequately skilled for *your* purposes? Try asking these practical questions when interviewing prospective interpreters:

- "Where were you trained?"

- "What are the credentials of your schools/teachers?"

- "What was the nature of your training" (i.e., German literature versus business German)?

- "How often do you work as a translator?" (Yes, foreign language skills *do* get rusty.)

- "Did you ever *live* in this foreign country?"

- "What were your last three translating assignments?" (Ask for specific details: lengths of assignments, types of material, types of clients, unusual circumstances, fees, et cetera. Be sure to request the names of these clients, so you can check for recent references.)

- "Have you ever served as an interpreter within my particular industry?" (This is a critical point. Each business has its own lingo, its own buzz words. You want someone who can translate your distinctive terminology like an "insider.")

In addition, ask *yourself* some questions:

- "Do I feel comfortable with this interpreter?" (Rapport is an important factor! After all, you've got to place a great deal of trust in your translator—and you want to do it with confidence.)

- "Will this person represent me well—in an attractive, well-groomed manner?" (Look at it this way: In the eyes of the audience, your interpreter is literally a stand-in for *you*.)

Here's a final caveat about using a translator—straight from the mouth of President Reagan.

In remarks to the National Governors' Association, President Reagan included this bit of self-deprecating humor about the pitfalls of speaking to a foreign audience:

> As you know, I recently visited Mexico to meet with President de la Madrid. And I was reminded of when I was governor of California and was asked by the then-President to go down and represent him. . . .
>
> On this first visit to Mexico, I gave a speech to a rather large audience and then sat down to rather unenthusiastic and scattered applause. I was embarrassed and tried to cover all of that, because what made it worse was that the next speaker up was speaking in Spanish, which I didn't understand, but he was getting interrupted virtually every line with most enthusiastic applause.
>
> So, I started clapping before anyone else and longer than anyone else until our ambassador learned over and said to me, "I wouldn't do that if I were you. He's interpreting your speech."

THE FINISHING TOUCHES

Consider all of the "little things" you can do to give your international speeches a special flair.

- When H. Norman Schwarzkopf was made an honorary member of the French Foreign Legion at a ceremony near Marseilles, he flattered his audience by delivering his most powerful line in French. Talking to the Foreign Legion officers, he used his best French accent to offer this heartfelt praise: "Your men are great."

- In his historic visit to Cuba at the age of seventy-seven, Pope John Paul delivered his homily in Spanish—and the crowds responded enthusiastically with the sounds of maracas and drums set to Roman Catholic prayers filling the air.

- When Steve Harlan, vice chairman, international, of KPMG Peat Marwick, addressed the benefits of free trade with Mexico, he concluded with an old Mexican proverb. First, he delivered the proverb in its original Spanish, "El que adelante no mira, atras se queda." Then, he paused a moment and offered its English translation, "He who doesn't look ahead, stays behind." By offering the foreign proverb in both languages, he created a more dramatic rapport with his international audience.

FOURTEEN

Speakers Bureaus

✳

It is generally better to deal by speech than by letter.
—Francis Bacon, lord chancellor of England.

Do these situations sound familiar?

- You're a manager at an electric utility, and customers are worried about the possibility of transmission lines causing cancer. How can you convince the community that your operations are safe?

- You're an administrator at a hospital, you've just expanded your outpatient services, and you'd like more people to know about your new facilities. What's the best way to reach potential patients?

- You're a branch manager at a bank, and you need to pursue new customers more aggressively. How can you persuade people to use the wide spectrum of financial services you offer?

- You're a senior vice president at a telephone company, and you'd like to inform consumers about rapid changes in the telecommunications industry. What's the best way to create community awareness and goodwill?

Consider using a *speakers bureau*. A speakers bureau is an *organized* effort to communicate a company's message to specific target groups—perhaps to the Rotary, or to the Chamber of Commerce, or to women's groups, men's clubs, or school groups.

More and more companies are finding that speakers bureaus are an effective, low-cost way to reach a variety of civic, business, professional, social, and educational organizations—in short, to present their corporate message to important constituencies within their community.

Pharmaceutical companies, utilities, oil companies, hospitals, and nonprofit groups—these are just a few of the organizations that have benefited by running effective speakers bureaus.

If you'd like to set up a brand-new speakers bureau for your company . . . or if you'd like to pump some life into an inactive bureau . . . or if you'd like to correct some specific problems with an ineffective bureau . . . read on. These guidelines should help.

MEMBERSHIP

Who can become a member of your speakers bureau? Consider your options:

- Any current employee?

- Either part-time or full-time?

- Both union and management?

- From entry-level to upper management?

- How about the company's retirees? (They typically know the company well, are quite aware of industry issues, have time to donate, enjoy sharing their expertise, and can prove quite credible to audiences.)

SIZE

How large should you make your bureau? Answer: Only as large as you can manage.

After all, what's the sense in having seventy-five members listed with your speakers bureau if you can't book enough speaking engagements to keep them all involved, or if you can't find enough time to supervise each speaker?

A better option: Keep the bureau small, and do a more efficient job of managing each speaker's special talents.

It takes a lot of effort to run a speakers bureau. Too often, top management thinks a speakers bureau can be managed as a part-time chore— dumped on the newest person in PR, or pushed onto a secretary's desk. That's a misconception.

Consider the risks if you

- book a date improperly

- choose the wrong speaker for a particular audience

- have an assigned speaker get sick at the last minute

- forget to check audiovisual needs

- provide wrong handouts

- send out an unprepared, uninteresting speaker

- fail to inform bureau members about changes in company policies

If you don't keep on top of these logistics, you'll discourage your speakers, alienate your audiences, and create alarm among top management. Prevent problems by making sure your bureau has the full-time coordinator it deserves.

TRAINING

Your speakers will be only as good as the training they get. So, decide up-front *how* you wish to train them, and *how often*.

Again, what's the use of having seventy-five members in your bureau if you can't get the budget to train all of them effectively?

Much smarter: Match the size of your membership to your training budget. If you can get only enough money to train forty members each year, then be realistic. Limit the size of your bureau to that number. Better to train forty members well than to train seventy-five members poorly. Don't try to "stretch" your dollars by skipping training sessions—that's no bargain.

PAYMENT/BENEFITS

Will you pay your members for each speech they give? That can be risky.

Wise speakers bureaus generally avoid monetary payment because there are too many variables and too many pitfalls. After all, would it be fair to pay a mediocre speaker the same as a terrific speaker? Would evening or weekend speeches demand higher rates? Would hostile audiences merit larger fees? (If so, who's to define a hostile audience?)

Perhaps most important, would a "paid" speaker have as much credibility with an audience as a member who simply volunteers to speak from personal commitment? Remember: Audiences are quick to spot a "hired gun"—and often respond accordingly.

A smarter choice: Offer your speakers *other* forms of compensation. After members have given a significant number of speeches, consider offering some extra vacation time, a complementary makeover session that will improve their podium appearance, the opportunity to take advanced courses in presentation skills, or even a simple, heartfelt "thank you" letter (and the knowledge that their efforts will be recognized in upcoming performance reviews).

You'll also need to address the whole issue of expense accounts. Decide *in advance* if you'll reimburse your speakers for taxi fares, car mileage, and restaurant meals. Just as important, decide *in advance* what your limits will be. (Otherwise, you might find yourself paying speakers too much money to dine in fancy restaurants.)

MOTIVATION

Once you've got your members signed up, how can you keep them interested? Consider setting up a simple point system, giving speakers credit for the:

- number of speeches they give

- number of recruits they sign up

- number of new forums they find

With a simple chart, your members can see—at a glance—how their activity level compares with that of other speakers. Put a star by the names of speakers who meet a certain level of productivity.

When Seattle City Light began giving its speakers credit for the number of presentations they gave, the bureau's bookings shot up dramatically—literally quadrupling in the first year! The bureau's coordinator sends quarterly performance reports to all layers of management—creating a higher profile for her speakers and fostering companywide support for the good work of the bureau.

RECOGNITION/REWARDS

Let's face it: When employees give up a Saturday afternoon to speak at a community event on the company's behalf, when they trudge out in a snowstorm to honor a speaking engagement at the Lion's Club, or when they drop what they're doing to "fill in" as a last-minute speaker at the Rotary—well, don't you think they deserve some special recognition?

Here are some ideas:

- Host an annual breakfast, luncheon, or dinner for all of the bureau's members. Let your budget determine the meal and the restaurant you choose. Remember: A first-rate breakfast is seen as more luxurious than a third-rate dinner. If you're working with a shoestring budget, skip the restaurant and offer a simple buffet in-house. By using local delis and caterers, you can keep your costs to a minimum.

- Treat your most productive speakers to a special event—perhaps theater tickets, a concert, or a day's pass to a theme park. Allow them to bring along a spouse or friend to make up for all those times when their speaking assignments kept them away from home.

- Hire a motivational speaker to address the bureau at an annual gathering. This appearance by a professional speaker will not only serve as a reward but also will "rev up" the bureau's members for their own assignments.

Utilities, hospitals, and a wide range of organizations often ask me to speak at their recognition dinners. On these occasions, I make my speeches both informational and motivational—with a good dose of humor. (For example, a typical topic might be: "How to Write and Give a Speech—and Survive!") My goal? To give the bureau members an enjoyable evening—and also inspire them to improve their own speeches.

- Ask the CEO to send your members a personal letter of appreciation. An added touch: Frame the letter, so members can put it on display.

- Send a holiday gift. Include a personal note of appreciation.

The Baptist Medical Centers in Birmingham, Alabama, run a Health Talks speakers bureau that consists of BMC physicians and other health-care professionals. Each December, the coordinator sends a small gift of appreciation (perhaps a potted plant, or a practical desk accessory) to her speakers. To keep costs down, she distributes the token gifts through interoffice mail.

PERFORMANCE STANDARDS

There's no sense in giving speeches unless you know they're accomplishing something. If you provide your audiences with an evaluation form, you'll gain valuable information about the success (or failure) of your bureau's presentations.

Be sure to keep your evaluation forms simple. If you make them complex and time-consuming, no one will bother to fill them out—and you'll lose valuable insights into the effectiveness of your speakers bureau.

A simple evaluation form would include these basics:

- Speaker? ____excellent____good____fair____poor

- Content? ____useful____not relevant to my needs

- What did you like best about the program? _____
_____

- Can you suggest any changes? _____
_____

- What topics would you like to see in the future? _____
_____

* Are you active in any other groups that might like to hear one of our free presentations? _____

(If so, please give your name, phone number, and e-mail so we can contact you:) _____

LETTING THE COMMUNITY KNOW ABOUT YOUR PROGRAMS

It doesn't do much good to have terrific speakers in your bureau if no one knows about them. So, make it a priority to publicize your bureau's programs.

Start by putting information on your company's Web site. Then prepare a brochure. It needn't be big or glossy or expensive—just effective. List the members of your speaking team, and cite their credentials. If possible, provide photographs of your speakers—but make sure they're *good* photos (not some blurry, boring head shots you've had lying around the office for the past decade).

Mail the brochure to all the potential groups in your area. (The Chamber of Commerce usually has such a listing.) Call the program chairperson of each group. With luck, you might be able to line up speaking engagements on the spot. At the very least, you can make a friendly contact and follow up another time.

Ask your speakers to help publicize the bureau's Web site—perhaps at their church, or at their monthly Lion's Club meeting, or in their doctor's office. The possibilities are virtually unlimited.

Be sure to send short press releases to all the local newspapers. The editors may well be able to list your programs in their "community calendar" sections.

APPROPRIATE FORUMS

When you're just starting your speakers bureau, you'll welcome almost any audience—just to give your speakers something to do!

But, as you receive more speaking invitations, you'll become increasingly choosy about your audiences. After all, you simply won't have enough time to accept every invitation that comes your way.

How to pick and choose the best forums for your purposes? Consider:

- *Size.* (Will the audience be large enough to justify your expenditure of time, effort, and money?)

- *Type of meeting.* (Women's club luncheon? Professional panel meeting? Civic forum? Community event? Senior citizen social gathering? Ask yourself, "Will this meeting give us an *appropriate* forum to deliver our message?")

- *Typical speaker.* (Ask: "Who spoke at last month's meeting? And the month before that?" You'll gain some insights into the type of programs they run—and the type of attention or inattention you can expect from this particular audience.)

- *Agenda.* (What other activities will be part of the program? Who else will be speaking, entertaining, fundraising, recruiting, et cetera, at this event? For example, if you've been asked to talk to senior citizens about energy conservation, but the program's *main* event is a bingo game—well, read the writing on the wall, decline the invitation, and direct your efforts to an audience where you'll get a more attentive response and a better return on your speaking investment.)

FIFTEEN

Speechwriters: How to Hire One and How to Work with One

✳

We can't all do everything.
—Virgil

When Gerald Ratner, the world's largest jewelry retailer, gave a speech at London's Albert Hall, he offered these four rules to becoming a multimillionaire:

1. Understand your market.

2. Form clear quality goals.

3. Evaluate your product against the competition's.

4. Don't write your own speeches.

There's some truth in that last point!

The fact is: Very few senior executives have the *time* to write their own speeches. After all, it's simply not cost-effective for CEOs to spend weeks laboring over a speech when they should be doing what they're paid to do, which is *run a company*.

What's more, very few senior executives have the *inclination* to write their own speeches. They're business people—not writers—so it's only natural for them to be more comfortable managing business details than putting pen to paper (or, finger to keyboard).

And, yes, let's be brutally honest: Very, *very* few senior executives have the *talent* to write their own speeches. After all, speechwriting is a highly demanding specialty . . . so specialized, in fact, that most professional writers don't do it well. Why? Because the process of writing a speech is quite different from writing a memo, or a press release, or a newspaper story—and woe be to anyone who fails to grasp this vital difference.

So, if *you* think you would benefit from hiring the expertise of a professional speechwriter (either on staff or as a freelance/consultant), start by asking other business people for referrals. Then, use these practical questions to help choose someone who's right *for you.*

- "How long have you been writing speeches?"

  You want someone with experience . . . someone who has handled a great number of speechwriting assignments . . . someone who can approach virtually any speaking situation with skill, confidence, and aplomb.

- "Is speechwriting your specialty?"

  This is a critical factor. If the writer is a generalist—that is, someone who does press releases one day, brochures the next, and speeches whenever they come along—you simply won't get the benefit of a well-tuned speechwriter's "ear."

  Tip: The location of your business need not limit you. Even if you operate out of a small town, you still have access to top speechwriting talent. A phone, a FAX, and e-mail will connect you with talented speechwriters all over the country. So, don't limit yourself unnecessarily by imposing geographical restrictions.

- "Do you do all of the speechwriting yourself—or, do you subcontract some assignments?"

  I cannot stress this point enough. Beware of any firm that takes a "group approach" to speechwriting.

Case in point: Many public relations firms will try to impress the client by sending high-ranking representatives to preliminary meetings, but then secretly "farm out" the actual speechwriting job to an unidentified freelancer. Quite often, to cut corners, PR firms choose the least-expensive freelancers they can get—and then the client (who paid top dollar to get a big-name PR firm) wonders why the submitted speech looks so amateurish.

One other serious consideration: If a PR firm subcontracts its speeches to freelance writers you don't know, how can you be sure your material is being treated confidentially? How can you be sure the unseen and unscreened freelancers aren't also taking assignments from your competitors?

Again, you're always better off developing a one-on-one relationship with a professional speechwriter you can trust implicitly.

• "Who are your current or recent clients?"

• "Do you have long-standing relationships with your clients? For example, how many speeches have you done for the XYZ Corporation?"

• "What do you know about the issues my industry faces?"

  Professional speechwriters prepare for interviews by reading about your company and your industry. Accept nothing less.

• "What's your educational background?"

  Caution: Don't think speechwriters need a particular degree in communications, public relations, or journalism. That's a misconception.

  What matters is a bright mind, a keen understanding of the world, a knack for creative listening, an ability to learn new material quickly, a sensitivity about language, and a deep love for the spoken word.

* "What's your professional background?"

    Another caution: Nobody really *begins* a career as a speechwriter. No twenty-two-year-old, fresh out of college and lacking real-life business experience, steps into a speechwriting slot and simply keeps moving up the speechwriting ladder, decade after decade. (And if they did . . . well, frankly, I'd be highly suspicious of their too-narrow background!) Speechwriting is often the culmination of several dynamic career interests.

* "Can you offer constructive criticism?"

    No head-nodders who will say anything to please the boss! You're looking for a bright individual who can tell you what you're doing wrong with your speeches—and show you how to improve.

* "Can you work quickly?"

    Here's an all-too-common scenario:

    Over two months ago, you asked your PR department to write an important speech, but they got tied up producing the annual report or fielding media questions or dealing with an employee crisis . . . whatever.

    Anyhow, they waited until the last minute to write your speech, and now (not surprisingly!) their draft looks like it was slapped together during a lunch hour.

    You're dissatisfied. You're frustrated. You wanted a *terrific* speech for this important occasion, and now you're stuck—with only five days left.

    It's times like these when you're glad you've already got a freelance speechwriter listed in your address book—someone you can depend on to work quickly and produce a quality manuscript. Treat this person like gold.

    If you *don't* already know a speechwriter like this, resolve to start interviewing *now* so you'll never be caught unprepared again.

- "Would you provide recommendations from your clients?"

  Be specific. Ask for names and titles. For example, a beginning speechwriter might brag that he's worked for "many executives at Fortune 50 companies"—when, in fact, he did only one actual assignment involving a group of mid-level managers. Learn to probe for references and honest responses.

- "Would you show me some samples of your work?"

  Warning: Truly professional speechwriters do *not* pass out samples casually. They're discreet. They consider their speeches to be the property of their clients. So, respect their professionalism and don't ask to see any confidential material.

  A much better alternative: Speechwriters can provide *excerpts* of recent speeches, or they can individually ask their clients for permission to distribute a particular manuscript.

- "Do your speeches get media coverage?"

  Top speechwriters know how to write attention-getting speeches that prove irresistibly quotable to reporters. Their speeches are often reprinted in *Vital Speeches*, or quoted in the *New York Times*, or cited in significant trade publications.

  These speechwriters can help you get valuable media attention for your company—attention that will enhance your professional status, promote your products, tout your services, build credibility for your organization, and draw attention to the issues of your industry.

  Not surprisingly, these speechwriters can command more money. They are well worth it.

- "Would you be willing to look at three of my recent speeches and offer a critique?"

  Naturally, since you're asking a professional writer to do professional work, you need to offer payment.

Only a nonprofessional would accept an assignment without pay.

• "Would you accept a short speechwriting assignment so I can see the way we'd work together?"

It doesn't have to be a big speech, the first time around. Just assign something short—say, an introduction, or a retirement tribute, or an award presentation, something that will allow the two of you to work together as a team on an exploratory basis.

Again, you will need to pay for this initial assignment—perhaps not top dollar, but certainly a respectable fee.

• "Would you describe your fee structure?"

You have a right to ask for cost estimates in advance. Your speechwriter may well offer you a price *range*, depending on how complex the assignment becomes. For example, if a speech requires two on-site meetings, it will cost more than if the same speech could be accomplished via phone and e-mail.

Remember: To your speechwriter, time *is* money. The more efficient and streamlined the process, the lower the total fee.

Consider also the deadline you're giving the speechwriter. The tighter the deadline, the greater the fee.

Experienced speechwriters are used to being brought in at the last minute, and they're used to working nights, weekends, and holidays to help clients beat a deadline. But, be aware: They *will* charge more for these rush assignments.

So, if you ask professional speechwriters to do some rush assignments over Thanksgiving weekend, they may well give up their holiday plans to accommodate you—but they'll charge accordingly.

And, come to think of it, you wouldn't have it any other way, would you?

APPENDIX: Useful Books, Web Sites, and Professional Organizations

❊ ─────────────────────────────────

To buy books would be a good thing if we also could buy the time to read them. As it is, the act of purchasing them is often mistaken for the assimilation and mastering of their content.

—Arthur Schopenhauer

BOOKS

Anecdotes

Bernard, Andre, and Clifton Fadiman. *The Bartlett's Book of Anecdotes,* revised edition. Boston: Little, Brown, 2001. An updated version of the *Little, Brown Book of Anecdotes,* this book will always hold a prime spot on my bookshelf. It offers well-researched anecdotes about thousands of famous people through the ages—from Neil Armstrong and Bob Dole to Dorothy Parker and Xerxes. Valuable subject index, source list, and bibliography. You can count on this book for excellent material on a wide range of topics.

Boller, Paul F. Jr. *Presidential Anecdotes.* New York: Oxford University Press, 1996 (revised). Detailed anecdotes covering everything from taxes to military strategy.

Hughes, R. Kent. *1001 Great Stories and Quotes.* Wheaton, IL: Tyndale House, 1998. The author, a pastor, offers a broad collection of inspirational and humorous anecdotes.

Biographical Quotations

Morris, Desmond. *The Book of Ages.* New York: Penguin, 1983. This book has been around a long while, but it's still a terrific source if you want to say a few clever words at someone's birthday party.

- *Age fifty:* "For certain people, after fifty, litigation takes the place of sex." (Gore Vidal)

- *Age seventy:* "To be seventy years young is sometimes far more cheerful and hopeful than to be forty years old." (Oliver Wendell Holmes)

Ratcliffe, Susan, ed. *People on People: The Oxford Dictionary of Biographical Quotations.* New York, NY: Oxford University Press, 2001. Want to learn "who said what" about Margaret Thatcher, or Picasso, or anybody else, for that matter? Start here. You'll get pithy quotes—with solid documentation.

Sampson, Anthony, and Sally Sampson. *The Oxford Book of Ages.* New York: Oxford University Press, 1988. Quotations and poetry about every year of life.

- "I'd like to go on being thirty-five for a long time." (Margaret Thatcher)

- "When you come to write my epitaph, Charles, let it be in these delicious words, 'She had a long twenty-nine.'" (Rosalind in James Barrie's *Rosalind*)

- "I'm fifty-three years old and six feet four. I've had three wives, five children and three grandchildren. I love good whiskey. I still don't understand women, and I don't think there is any man who does." (John Wayne)

Birthday Celebrations and Anniversaries

Lewman, David. *"When I Was Your Age . . .".* Chicago: Triumph Books, 1997. Remarkable achievements of writers, artists, and musicians—from age one to one hundred. Where else could you learn that Tony Bennett became cool all over again at sixty-six when he presented an

MTV Music Video Award, and Grandma Moses had her first New York City art show at age seventy-nine?

Business

Boone, Louis E. *Quotable Business.* New York: Random House, 1992. Over 2,800 funny, irreverent, and insightful quotations about corporate life, including:

* *Accounting:* "Specialists in finance must be on tap, but they should never be on top." (Al Newharth)

* *Strategy:* "In baiting a mouse trap with cheese, always leave room for the mouse." (Saki, a.k.a. H. H. Munro)

Eigen, Lewis, and Jonathan Siegel. *The Manager's Book of Quotations.* New York: AMACOM, 1989. Well-researched quotations covering forty-seven topics:

* *Rules, Red Tape, and Bureaucracy:* "We can overcome gravity, but sometimes the paperwork is overwhelming." (Wernher Von Braun, pioneer rocket scientist)

* *Strategic Thinking:* "There is no security on this earth; there is only opportunity." (Douglas MacArthur)

Woods, John. *The Quotable Executive.* New York: McGraw-Hill, 2000. It contains excellent biographical identification.

Calendar or Daily Listings

Dickson, Paul. *Timelines: Day by Day and Trend by Trend from the Dawn of the Atomic Age to the Gulf War.* Reading, Massachusetts: Addison Wesley Publishing, 1991. This is the best book of its kind. Suppose your organization was founded in 1971, and you want to find interesting details about that year. This book offers great tidbits that can make any presentation more interesting. In 1971, for example:

- The term "workaholic" worked itself into the language.

- The first handheld calculator was marketed for $249.

- Smiley-faced buttons popped up everywhere.

- The London Bridge was moved to the Arizona desert.

- The People's Republic of China became a member of the United Nations.

Mason, Eileen. *Witty Words.* New York: Sterling Publishing, 1992. An excellent way to find out what happened in history on May 17 or August 12, or whenever you happen to be speaking. You'll get great quips for:

- *Blame Someone Else Day:* "The man who can smile when things go wrong has thought of someone he can blame it on." (Arthur Bloch)

- *Canada Day:* "Quebec is one of the ten provinces against which Canada is defending itself." (Carl Dubuc)

- *Lawyers' Day:* "A chi consiglia, no duole il capo." (Italian saying; "He who gives the counsel doesn't get the headaches.")

- *Save Your Vision Week:* "No one is ever so blind as not to be able to see another person's duty." (Anonymous)

Careers

Evans, William R., and Andrew Frothingham. *Well-Done Roasts.* New York: St. Martin's Press, 1992. This book includes zingers about:

- *Editors:* "I share Adlai Stevenson's opinion of editors. He said, 'An editor is a man who separates the wheat from the chaff and prints the chaff.'"

- *Psychiatrists:* "A psychiatrist is a man who goes to the Follies Bergère and looks at the audience."

- *Retirement:* "We're not sure what we'll do without him . . . but we've been thinking about it for years."

Pasta, Elmer. *Complete Books of Roasts, Toasts, and Boasts.* West Nyack, NY: Parker Publishing, 1982. It's an old book, but invaluable because it covers an extraordinarily broad selection of jobs—from acupuncturist and beekeeper, to genealogist, lifeguard, trapeze artist and X-ray technician. It's great for retirement tributes.

Simpson, James B., and Daniel J. Boorstin. *Simpson's Contemporary Quotations*. Boston: Houghton Mifflin, 1988. It features separate chapters giving lively comments about a variety of occupations (military officers, doctors, lawyers, reporters, entertainers, restaurateurs). Excellent documentation.

Colleges and Universities

Bronner, Simon J. *Piled Higher and Deeper: The Folklore of Campus Life*. You'll find well-researched folklore dealing with campus issues like final exams, absentminded professors, fraternity pledging, and faculty quirks. Where else could you learn about:

* the parody of the application form at the University of Pittsburgh

* freshman hazing

* campus drinking games

* mnemonic devices

Commencements

Ross, Alan, ed. *Speaking of Graduation*. Nashville, TN: Walnut Grove Press, 2001. Excerpts from graduation speeches—both serious and humorous.

Definitions

Brussell, Eugene E. *Webster's New World Dictionary of Quotable Definitions*. Englewood Cliffs, New Jersey: Prentice-Hall, 1988. This book is worth its weight in gold for any speaker. Need a clever definition? Forget your regular dictionary. Instead, turn to this book for more than 17,000 lively definitions on 2,000 subjects.

- *Exercise:* "A modern superstition, invented by people who ate too much and had nothing to think about." (George Santayana)

- *Inflation:* "Too much money going to somebody else." (William Vaughan)

- *Public relations:* "Hiring someone who knows what he is doing to convince the public that you know what you are doing." (Hyman Maxwell Berston)

- *San Francisco:* "A city of four seasons every day." (Bob Hope)

Design and Typography Techniques

Williams, Robin. *The Non-Designers Design Book.* Berkeley, California: Peachpit Press, 1994. Want to make your slides look better? Create more attractive handouts? You will learn a great deal in this book. And your presentation materials will improve dramatically.

Entertainment

Crofton, Ian, and Donald Fraser. *A Dictionary of Musical Quotations.* New York, NY: Schirmer Books, 1985. Old—but an invaluable source of quotations about all aspects of music: opera, electronic music, folk music, performers, conductors, and composers ranging from Bach to Wagner.

Rees, Nigel. *Cassell's Movie Quotations.* London: Cassell, 2000. Great lines from the movies, from moviemakers, and from movie fans. Outstanding resource.

Environment and Ecology

Rodes, Barbara K., and Odell Rice. *A Dictionary of Environmental Quotations.* Baltimore: The Johns Hopkins University Press, 1992. One of the few places to find good quotations about the environment.

- "This planet is not private property." (Hazel Henderson)

- "If people destroy something replaceable made by mankind, they are called vandals; if they destroy something irreplaceable made by God, they are called developers." (Joseph Wood Krutch)

Ethnic and Regional

De Ley, Gerd. *African Proverbs.* New York: Hippocrene Books, 1999. An excellent volume, offering material that isn't easily found elsewhere. Very well organized. It identifies proverbs by country, by province, and even by tribe. Provides photos, a helpful bibliography, and an appendix with information on various tribes.

Jones, Loyal, and Billy Edd Wheeler. *Laughter in Appalachia: A Festival of Southern Mountain Humor.* Little Rock, Arkansas: August House Publishers, 1987. Anecdotes about doctors, lawyers, schools, religion, and politics. [Note: August House prides itself on an outstanding American Folklore Series, representing about a dozen cultures. For a catalog, contact August House Publishers, Inc., P.O. Box 3223, Little Rock, Arkansas 72203.]

O'Farrell, Padraic. *Irish Toasts, Curses and Blessings.* New York: Sterling, 1995. Absolutely wonderful entries. My favorite?

- "May you never see a bad day—and if it sees you, may it be wearing glasses."

Sherman, Josepha. *A Sampler of Jewish American Folklore.* Little Rock, Arkansas: August House Publishers, 1992. Wit and wisdom from the Old World to the New. Some chapters deal with ceremonial topics (birth, marriage, and death). Other chapters provide humorous stories, proverbs, riddles, and clever folktales. Especially helpful: detailed notes and a bibliography.

Telushkin, Joseph. *Uncommon Wisdom.* New York: Shapolsky Publishers, 1987. This book offers seldom-seen Talmudic blessings, Biblical stories, and rabbinical observations. It also has wonderful quips from popular contemporary sources. It's divided into sections based on the traditional categories of Jewish commandments: "between man and man" and "between man and God."

- "I don't want to achieve immortality through my work. I want to achieve it through not dying." (Woody Allen)

- "Too bad that all the people who know how to run the country are busy driving taxicabs and cutting hair." (George Burns)

Weinrich, Beatrice Silverman. *Yiddish Folktales.* New York: Pantheon Books, 1988. Almost 200 marvelous tales from the world of East European Jewry. *Special Note:* The Pantheon Fairy Tale and Folklore Library also publishes great collections of folklore from Africa, Japan, Ireland, and elsewhere.

West, John O. *Mexican-American Folklore.* Little Rock, Arkansas: August House Publishers, 1988. Legends, riddles, songs, tales of saints, and stories of revolutionaries. Especially useful is the chapter on proverbs, offered in both Spanish and English.

- "El que adelante no mira, atras se queda." (He who doesn't look ahead stays behind.)

Eulogies

McNees, Pat, ed. *Dying: A Book of Comfort.* New York: Warner Books, 1998. A diverse collection of quotations and literary passages about the subject of death, and a valuable resource for anyone of any faith who must deliver a eulogy.

Food

Cader, Michael, with Debby Roth. *Eat These Words.* New York: Harper-Collins, 1991. A tiny book, filled with great fun. Where else could you find:

- "Sex is good, but not as good as fresh sweet corn." (Garrison Keillor)

- "In England, there are sixty different religions, but only one sauce." (Voltaire)

Egerton, March, ed. *Since Eve Ate Apples.* Portland, Oregon: Tsunami Press, 1994. An outstanding reference book for anyone who cares about dining. The book is well organized, with 161 categories arranged alphabetically, all quotations presented chronologically, and excellent source notations.

- "Security is a smile from a headwaiter." (Russell Baker)

- "In New Orleans, food is like sex. Everybody's interested." (Ella Brennan)

- "As a child, my family's menu consisted of two choices: Take it, or leave it." (Buddy Hackett)

History

Axelrod, Alan. *The Quotable Historian.* New York: McGraw-Hill, 2000. It contains dozens of thematic sections.

Frost, Elizabeth. *The Bully Pulpit.* New York: Facts on File, 1988. If you want presidential quotes, go here first. This is your best source.

Mencken, H. L. *A New Dictionary of Quotations.* New York: Knopf, 1987. A truly excellent volume. Superbly researched, carefully annotated, and well organized. In spite of the huge size, you can find things easily. It provides the thoughts of major figures in history and literature.

Humor

Jones, Loyal, and Billy Edd Wheeler. *Hometown Humor, U.S.A.* Little Rock, Arkansas: August House Publishers, 1991. It presents country humor on a wide range of topics: aging, health, farmers, education, law, politics, preachers, and city folks.

Metcalf, Fred. *The Penguin Dictionary of Modern Humorous Quotations.* London: Penguin, 1986. A decidedly British bent. The strong European references make this particularly useful.

- *Europe:* "European Community institutions have produced European beets, butter, cheese, wine, veal, and even pigs. But they have not produced Europeans." (Louise Weiss)

- *France:* "France is a place where the money falls apart in your hands, but you can't tear the toilet paper." (Billy Wilder)

- *London:* "When it's three o'clock in New York, it's still 1938 in London." (Bette Midler)

Pentz, Croft M. *The Complete Book of Zingers.* Wheaton, Illinois: Tyndale House Publishers, 1990. The author is an Assemblies of God minister who set out to compile a witty collection of "one-sentence sermons." He succeeded. The wide range of topics includes:

- *Determination:* "Trying times are no time to quit trying."

- *Illness:* "Virus is a Latin word used by doctors to mean, 'Your guess is as good as mine.' "

- *Work:* "Pray to God, but row for shore."

Perret, Gene, and Linda Perret. *Funny Business.* Englewood Cliffs, New Jersey: Prentice-Hall, 1990. This is an indispensable book, with terrific one-liners that cover just about everything in the business world. It even has a funny section of quips on "Office Air-Conditioning." Now, what more could any business speaker ask for?

- Cheap bosses

- Advertising

- Seminars

- Office collections

- Personnel

- Resumes

- Mandatory retirement

- Executive perks

- Memo writing

- Job Application Forms

Rees, Nigel. *Cassel Dictionary of Humorous Quotations.* New York: Sterling Publishing, 1998. It has great quips about:

- *Lawmaking:* "If you like laws and sausages, you should never watch either one being made." (Prince Otto von Bismarck)

- *Saving:* "Saving is a very fine thing, especially when your parents have done it for you." (Winston Churchill)

- *Schedule:* "There cannot be a crisis next week. My schedule is already full." (Henry Kissinger)

Law

Shrager, David, and Elizabeth Frost. *The Quotable Lawyer.* New York: Facts on File, 1986. Well-researched quotes on the law—from ancient times to the present, with an index of subjects and of authors.

Military

Charlton, James. *The Military Quotation Book.* New York: St. Martin's Press, 1990. Great lines—witty, pithy, and short. Ideal for sales presentations and sports banquets. However, it doesn't have a subject index.

- "War is too important to be left to the generals." (George Clemenceau)

- "The mere absence of war is not peace." (John F. Kennedy)

- "In war, there is no second prize for the runner up." (General Omar Bradley)

Politics and Government

Baker, Daniel B. *Power Quotes.* Detroit: Gale Research, 1992. You'll find 4,000 trenchant sound bites about every aspect of politics and government. It's well researched, with outstanding source information.

Torricelli, U.S. senator Robert. *Quotations for Public Speakers.* New Brunswick, NJ: Rutgers University Press, 2001. This is a historical, literary, and political anthology—with topics ranging from diplomacy to justice to urban affairs.

Predictions

Lee, Laura. *Bad Predictions: 2000 Years of the Best Minds Making the Worst Forecasts*. Rochester, MI: Elsewhere Press, 2000. Where else could you find these gems?

- "Law will be simplified [during the next century]. Lawyers will have diminished, and their fees will have been vastly curtailed." (Junius Henri Browne, journalist, 1893)

- "By the year 2000, we will live in a paperless society." (Roger Smith, GM chairman, 1986)

- "Who would want to see a play about an unhappy traveling salesman?" (Cheryl Crawford, Broadway producer, 1948, in rejecting Arthur Miller's drama *Death of a Salesman*)

Quotations

Allen, Jessica. *Quotable Men of the Twentieth Century*. New York: William Morrow and Company, 1999. The book covers a wide range of contemporary topics, from bureaucracy to technology.

Camp, Wesley D. *What a Piece of Work Is Man!* Englewood Cliffs, New Jersey: Prentice-Hall, 1990. Hard-to-find quotations from 2000 B.C. to the present. It's well organized and well documented with a phenomenal range of topics:

- *Profit.* "The engine which drives Enterprise is not thrift, but profit." (John Maynard Keynes)

- *Retirement.* "I married him for better or for worse, but not for lunch." (Hazel Weiss, after her husband retired as general manager of the Yankees)

- *Science.* "There is a lurking fear that some things are not meant to be known, that some inquiries are too dangerous for human beings to make." (Carl Sagan)

Ehrlich, Eugene, and Marshal deBruhl. *The International Thesaurus of Quotations.* New York: HarperCollins, 1996. This is a truly comprehensive research tool with over 16,000 entries, spanning 2,500 years and covering 1,000 subject categories. It offers an outstanding index of authors, an index of key words, and an index of categories.

- *Retirement:* "Cessation of work, not accompanied by cessation of expenses." (Cato the Elder, second century B.C.)

Frank, Leonard Roy. *Quotionary.* New York: Random House, 2001. This is a huge collection—particularly strong in contemporary sources.

- *Longevity:* "I attribute it to red meat and gin." (Julia Child)

Platt, Suzy, ed. *Respectfully Quoted.* New York. Barnes & Noble Books, 1993. It contains a wealth of classical and modern quotations, international in scope and conveniently indexed by subject, author, and keyword. Backed by solid research, it offers helpful historical notes for each quotation.

Rawson, Hugh. *Unwritten Laws: The Unofficial Rules of Life.* New York: Crown, 1998. Catchy slogans and one-liners.

- "Nine-tenths of wisdom consists in being wise in time." (Theodore Roosevelt)

- "Money isn't everything as long as you have enough." (Malcolm Forbes)

Rees, Nigel. *Brewer's Quotations: A Phrase and Fable Dictionary.* New York: Sterling Publishing, 1995. This wonderful book contains "the most commonly misquoted, misattributed, misascribed, misremembered, and most disputed sayings that there are"—and puts them in their proper historical context. An outstanding index.

Shanahan, John M., ed. *The Most Brilliant Thoughts of All Time.* New York: HaperCollins Publishers, 1999. What makes this so great for speakers? The entries are very short (running two lines or less) so they'll fit easily into your message and sound conversational. Some favorites:

- "In the field of observation, chance favors the prepared mind." (Louis Pasteur)

- "You don't hold your own in the world by standing on guard, but by attacking and getting well hammered yourself." (George Bernard Shaw)

Swainson, Bill, ed. *Encarta Book of Quotations.* New York: St. Martin's Press, 2000. This is an outstanding reference work with more than 25,000 quotations—and a large number of context notes (giving additional background information). There's a strong emphasis on international figures from the last one hundred years.

Religion and Philosophy

Cook, John. *The Book of Positive Quotations.* Minneapolis: Fairview Press, 1993. Ideal for motivational speeches. Very well organized, so it's easy to find what you want. (For example, the chapter on "Acceptance" has eighteen sections, allowing you to target your material quickly.)

Freeman, Criswell. *The Book of Christmas Wisdom.* Nashville: Walnut Grove Press, 1999. The best place to find comments about Christmas—both sacred and secular.

Peck, M. Scott, M.D., *Abounding Grace.* Kansas City, Missouri: Andrews McNeel, 2000. Dr. Peck, author of the classic *The Road Less Traveled,* provides an inspirational collection of quotations about happiness, courage, compassion, purity, perseverance, courtesy, faith, goodness, love, respect, strength, and wisdom.

Tomlinson, Gerald. *Treasury of Religious Quotations.* Englewood Cliffs, New Jersey: Prentice-Hall, 1991. Organized into 149 topics (from achievement to values), then subdivided into thirty religions and beliefs (with hard-to-find entries from Mormonism and Islam). As an example, the "Leadership" category includes:

- *Christianity:* "Can the blind lead the blind? Shall they not both fall into the ditch?" (*Holy Bible,* Luke: 6:39)

- *Confucianism:* "He stands in the middle, and leans not to either side."

- *Judaism:* "In the place where there is already a leader, do not seek to become a leader. But in the place where there is no leader, strive thou to become a leader." (*Talmud,* Berakot 63a)

- *Taoism:* "Handle a large kingdom with as gentle a touch as if you were cooking small fish."

Well, Albert M., Jr. *Inspiring Quotations.* Nashville: Thomas Nelson, 1988. More than 3,000 quotes from leading evangelicals, poets, philosophers, etc. A strong emphasis on fundamental Christian concerns—with chapters ranging from "Abortion" to "World Peace."

Winokur, Jon. *Zen to Go.* New York: New York: New American Library, 1989. This book has sound bites of wisdom from an astonishing cross-section of thinkers. Any reference book that can cite comedian George Carlin in the same breath as Dag Hammarskjold gets my attention.

- "Learn your lines and don't trip over the furniture." (Spencer Tracy, advice to young actors)

- "How old would you be if you didn't know how old you was?" (Satchell Paige)

Science

Fripp, Jon, Michael Fripp, and Deborah Fripp. *Speaking of Science: Notable Quotes on Science, Engineering, and the Environment.* Eagle Rock, Virginia: LLH Technology Publishing, 2000. It's an essential reference and an interesting read. You'll find well-researched quotations about:

- *Evolution:* "Evolution is chaos with feedback." (Joseph Ford)

- *Flood control:* "Risk cannot be eliminated; therefore it must be managed." (Institution of Civil Engineers)

- *Mechanical engineering:* "Mechanics is the paradise of the mathematical sciences, because by means of it one comes to the fruits of mathematics." (Leonardo da Vinci)

Sports

Tomlinson, Gerald, ed. *Speaker's Treasury of Sports Anecdotes, Stories, and Humor.* Englewood Cliffs, New Jersey: Prentice-Hall, 1990. Covers seventy-two categories, with quotes from fifty-four different sports and activities. It also offers a sports calendar and birthday listings for famous athletes.

Statistics

Gaither, C. C., and A. E. Cavozov-Gaither. *Statistically Speaking.* Philadelphia: Institute of Physics Publishing, 1996. It's the most comprehensive collection of quotations pertaining to statistics. An extraordinary reference work—with detailed bibliography and indices. It has surprisingly wide range of chapters, including:

- *Data:* "It is a capital mistake to theorize before one has the data." (Sherlock Holmes, a character created by Arthur Conan Dayle)

- *Distributions:* "Normality is a myth; there never has, and never will be, a normal distribution." (R. C. Geary)

- *Graphics:* "You can draw a lot of curves through three graph points. You can extrapolate it a lot of ways." (Michael Crichton)

- *Statistician:* "Most of you would as soon be told that you are cross-eyed or knock-kneed as that you are destined to be a statistician." (Josiah Stamp)

Storytelling

Lipman, Doug. *The Storytelling Coach.* Little Rock, Arkansas: August House Publishers, 1995. The book provides helpful principles and motivational advice for communicating your stories—in the classroom, in the boardroom, from the pulpit, or from the stage.

Mooney, Bill, and David Holt. *The Storyteller's Guide.* Little Rock, Arkansas: August House Publishers, 1996. It's packed with well-chosen anecdotes, examples, and parables that illuminate the art of storytelling and features interviews with more than fifty experienced storytellers—including teachers, librarians, authors, actors, and clergymen. If you're thinking of becoming a storyteller, this is an excellent place to start.

Toasts, Roasts, and Special Occasions

Detz, Joan. *Can You Say a Few Words?* New York: St. Martin's Press, 1991. It presents practical speaking advice for special occasions, including:

- award ceremonies
- retirements
- sports banquets
- patriotic ceremonies
- anniversary tributes
- commencements
- eulogies

Diagram Group. *The Little Giant Encyclopedia of Toasts and Quotes.* New York: Sterling Publishing, 1998. Roasts for all occasions and toasts for weddings, anniversaries, graduations, retirements.

Evans, William R., III, and Andrew Frothingham. *Crisp Toasts.* New York: St. Martin's Press, 1992. Great quips for popular events (from New Year's to christenings to anniversaries).

Irwin, Dale. *The Everything Toasts Book.* Holbrook, MA: Adams Media, 2000. The book contains a toast for every special occasion.

McManus, Ed, and Bill Nicholas. *We're Roasting Harry Tuesday Night.* Englewood Cliffs, New Jersey: Prentice-Hall, 1988. How to plan, write, and conduct the business or social roast.

- "Harry was a consultant. That's a guy who quit work, but kept the breaks and lunch."
- "Harry doesn't personally have ulcers, but he is a carrier."

Weather

Freier, George D. *Weather Proverbs.* Tucson, Arizona: Fisher Books, 1989. Are you giving a presentation the same day as a blizzard? Is everyone still talking about yesterday's thunderstorm? This book can give you some clever tie-ins.

Weddings

Jeffrey, Barbara. *Wedding Speeches and Toasts.* Berkshire, England: Foulsham Publishing, 1999. Quotations, stories, and practical advice for anyone who has to speak at a wedding.

Women

Maggio, Rosalie. *Quotations by Women.* Boston: Beacon Press, 1996. Offers 16,000 quotations, covering an extraordinary range of subjects and an outstanding index of subjects and key lines.

- "You cannot shake hands with a clenched fist." (Indira Gandhi)

- "Democracy is not a spectator sport." (Marian Wright Edelman)

- "I don't waste time thinking, 'Am I doing it right?' I say, 'Am I doing it?' " (Georgette Mosbacher)

- "Suffering makes you deep. Travel makes you broad. In case I get my pick, I'd rather travel." (Judith Viorst)

Warner, Carolyn. *The Last Word.* Englewood Cliffs, NJ: Prentice-Hall, 1992. It covers women's voices from all fields: from Eleanor Roosevelt and Pearl Buck to Mary Kay Ash and Erma Bombeck. It even offers this wise tidbit from Miss Piggy: "Never eat more than you can lift." (Indeed.)

WEB SITES FOR SPEAKERS

American Indian Tales

- www.kstrom.net/isk/stories/myths.html (Native American stories and quotations)

Aphorisms, Proverbs, and Quotations

- www.aphorismsgalore.com (Wide-ranging categories: art and literature, science and religion, work and recreation, etc.)

- www.columbia.edu/acis/bartleby/bartlett (Outstanding reference sources: *Bartlett's Familiar Quotations, Simpson's Contemporary Quotations,* and many more)

- www.creativequotations.com (Quotes to spruce up speeches. Proverbs from more than 300 countries and cultures.)

- www.famous-quotations.com (Searchable by category, author, and country)

Biographical Information

- www.s9.com (You can search this biographical dictionary by birth years, death years, titles, professions, literary or artistic works, and key achievements.)

Dates in History

- http://dmarie.com/asp/history.asp?action=process (Fun trivia for birthdays and anniversaries—newspaper headlines, sports stories, pop songs, etc.)

- www.idea-bank.com (A particularly good "History Today" file that offers well-researched material for each day of the year. It's fee based, but worth it.)

- www.infoplease.com (Historical events tied to the date of your speech)

Dictionaries

- www.onelook.com (An outstanding collection of dictionaries and glossaries)

Index to the Internet

- www.lii.org (This librarians' index to the Internet is outstanding.)

Myths and Legends

- http://pubpages.unh.edu/~cbsiren/myth.html (It's organized by region and language groups and covers the world: from Burma, the Caribbean, and Egypt, to Thailand, Tibet, and Vietnam.)

- www.mythiccrossroads.com/site_map.htm (Aesop's fables; Arthurian legends; Norse, Greek, and Egyptian gods and goddesses; African tales; and a particularly good section on characters of the Wild West)

- www.mythsearch.com/index.html (Information on proverbs, blessings, holidays, and festivals)

Newspapers Around the World

- www.ecola.com
- www.thepaperboy.com

Speech Texts

- http://gos.sbc.edu (Supported by Sweet Briar College. Interesting speeches by prominent women.)

- www.historychannel.com (Speeches by business, political, and academic leaders)

- www.historyplace.com/speeches/porevious.htm (You'll find a wide assortment of speech texts: from St. Francis of Assisi's "Sermon to the Birds" to Lou Gehrig's "Farewell to Yankee Fans" to Bill Clinton's "I Have Sinned.")

• www.winstonchurchill.org (Speeches, quotations, and anecdotes of Winston Churchill)

U.S. History

• www.law.ou.edu/hist/ (Historical speeches and political documents— from the pre-Colonial era to the present)

PROFESSIONAL ORGANIZATIONS

American Library Association, 50 East Huron Street, Chicago, IL 60611, 800-545-2433, www.ala.org

American Society of Journalists and Authors, 1501 Broadway, Suite 302, New York, NY 10036, 212-997-0947, www.asja.org

International Association of Business Communicators, One Hallidie Plaza, Suite 600, San Francisco, CA 94102, 415-433-3400, www.iabc.com

National Association of Government Communicators, 10366 Democracy Lane, Suite B, Fairfax, VA 22030, 703-691-0377, www.nagc.org

National Black Public Relations Society, 6565 Sunset Blvd, Suite 301, Hollywood, CA 90028, 323-466-8221, www.nbprs.org

National Speakers Association, 1500 South Priest Drive, Tempe, AZ 85281, 480-968-2552, www.nsa.org

National Storytelling Association, P.O. Box 309, Jonesborough, TN 37659, 423-753-2171, www.storynet.org

NY Women in Communications, 355 Lexington Avenue, 17 Floor, New York, NY, 212-297-2133, www.nywici.org

Public Relations Society of America, 33 Irving Place, New York, NY 10003, 212-995-2230, www.prsa.org

Toastmasters International, 2200 North Grand Avenue, Santa Ana, CA 92711, www.toastmasters.org

Women Executives in Public Relations, FDR Station, P.O. Box 7657, New York, NY 10150, 212-750-7373, www.wepr.org

Index